SIXTY YEARS, THIRTY PERSPECTIVES

60
30

SIXTY YEARS, THIRTY PERSPECTIVES: IRELAND AND THE UNIVERSAL DECLARATION OF HUMAN RIGHTS

Edited and with a Foreword by Donncha O'Connell

SIXTY YEARS, THIRTY PERSPECTIVES

First published 2009
by New Island
2 Brookside
Dundrum Road
Dublin 14

www.newisland.ie

ISBN 978-1-84840-044-3

New Island received financial assistance from
The Arts Council (An Chomhairle Ealaíon), Dublin, Ireland.

British Library Cataloguing Data. A CIP catalogue record for this book is available from the British Library.

Printed in Spain by Castuera, Industrias Gráficas, S.A.

10 9 8 7 6 5 4 3 2 1

CONTENTS

ACKNOWLEDGMENTS

We at Amnesty International extend our sincerest thanks to Donncha O'Connell for his extremely generous contribution of time, energy and professional input.

Warm thanks also to Derek Speirs, who is always an inspiration.

This publication was made possible with funding from the Atlantic Philanthropies.

Special thanks within the Amnesty International team to Sorcha Tunney for project management and to Justin, Rosalind, Pippa and Noeleen.

FOREWORD

As one ideology is undermined by historical events, antithetical ideologies erupt in triumphalism, as if the death of one implies life for the others. Thus, the fall of the Berlin Wall in 1989 was heralded as a lease of life for neo-liberalism and, arguably, market fundamentalism. The sudden collapse of under-regulated financial markets in 2008 will, no doubt, bring new hopes of revival for social democracy, underscored, with some tangible poignancy, by the election to the US presidency of Barack Obama. The world is struggling crazily with hope and despair. It is important to keep both alive.

Human rights – as articulated so brilliantly in the 1948 Universal Declaration of Human Rights – act as a fulcrum for the ideological scale that seems so susceptible to pendular historical swings. Although dogged by the inescapable problem of meaning – sometimes to the point of becoming a trendy 'new civic religion' – human rights provide a discursive framework for the resolution of humanity's problems that can be both civilised and civilising. This is a rich dividend for those of us who are stakeholders in the *now* that will become history.

Of course, there are myriad reasons to suspect that the beautiful words of the declaration are no more than that. Cost-benefit analyses applied to something like the UDHR are certainly speculative and probably futile. In this collection of essays, commissioned and selected by Amnesty International Ireland, you will find an appropriate mix of hope and despair that never yields to cynicism. Each of the authors, whose styles are as varied as their backgrounds, brings a wealth of experiential insight to the part of the declaration they have been asked to write about. The worlds of activism, public policy, law, religion, academia, sport and culture are all represented in this collection. Some of the contributors defy and transcend easy categorisation. It has been a privilege to work with all of them.

The pro-human rights consensus evident in this collection, notwithstanding differences in emphasis and grounding philosophies, is probably not indicative of a wider societal compact other than one informed by indifference or shallow acceptance. Many of the ideas promoted in these essays and many of their underlying assumptions – which, to the authors, seem self-evident – would be hotly contested by others who engage seriously and not so seriously with human rights debates.

In recent years, one of the biggest favours done for the human rights community was the full-frontal challenge to our role and responsibilities articulated so trenchantly by Michael McDowell in his various manifestations as Attorney General, Minister for Justice, Equality and Law Reform, and leader of the political party that was the Progressive Democrats. He was not without support that spanned the scales of form and taste from eminent to populist, sometimes in the same personage. In many respects, what McDowell and his supporters had to say about what they described as the 'so-called human rights community' was an appeal to a base level of populist sentiment, a deeply conservative and narrow view of democracy that could morph into an exhortation to political incorrectness, but one disguised as a plausible challenge to 'political correctness gone mad'. Its plausibility was given added value by an apparently robust embrace of civil and political rights that, by any international comparison, would be quaintly inchoate.

This kind of provocation can be useful so long as the tendency towards *ad hominem* comment doesn't become some kind of entertaining but pointless rhetorical boomerang. So let us engage with this powerful challenge to our human rights assumptions.

Why is it controversial or, indeed, undemocratic to suggest that socio-economic rights should be justiciable or amenable to vindication by recourse to judicial or quasi-judicial redress mechanisms? Why is it presumptuous of the vital forces of civil society, as represented by non-governmental organisations (NGOs), to be assertive in the promotion of their values and openly critical of government and the state, domestically and internationally? Why is it useful to have independent statutory bodies in the hazardous space between the state and the non-governmental sector charged with keeping government honest about its human rights obligations?

These are central questions in any human rights discourse that invite a plurality of answers all framed by different understandings of democracy.

To argue that recourse to the courts to vindicate socio-economic rights is some kind of an attempt to bypass the normal political processes, by achieving a judicial (and thereby profoundly undemocratic) intervention in the policy arena, ignores the fact that such recourse is sought, usually as a last resort, as a result of endemic failures in political processes to address the adverse condition of marginalised people. This cause-and-effect relationship is simply ignored on the assumption that some notional equality of power exists within political processes, but this is, demonstrably, nonsense. The ascription of dubious democratic values to those who argue for some right of corrective recourse to the courts to vindicate socio-economic rights, however residual and qualified, is surely a case of 'protesting too much' on the part of those who clearly elevate a particular view of the separation of powers, beyond a mere means of attaining the rule of law, to a superordinate and self-serving principle of constitutionalism.

For many reasons, representatives of NGOs tend to see right through this kind of legal sophistry. The subtle control of professional consensus, especially when laid down with the authority of judicial imprimatur, is thankfully absent from the NGO sector. By the same token, fidelity to missions or 'our own orthodoxies' – sometimes articulated in an apparently uncomplicated and reductive manner, having been through the wash of strategic and business planning – can be a diversion from the important and serious issues thrown up by such debates. This can be exacerbated when protagonists from 'the other side' engage in disparagement and personal commentary, prompting a degree of defensiveness that minimises the possibility of real engagement.

There is a worthwhile debate to be had about the justiciability of socio-economic rights – so let's have it! Let us examine our international human rights obligations seriously, with a view to their application in the domestic sphere, in a way that faithfully reflects the informing principles of universality and indivisibility that are so central to the international system for the protection of human rights. Now is the worst possible time for countries like Ireland to behave like 'slacker states' in the fulfilment of international human rights obligations.

Democratic space must be opened up to take account of the necessarily complicated ways in which power is dispersed and shared in modern states, never forgetting in whose name power is exercised – The People.

The dismantling by the Irish government in 2008 of vitally important elements of the human rights and equality infrastructure, by means of disproportionate budget cuts and other stratagems designed to undermine and subvert their impact, is depressing at many levels. However, it also presents opportunities for non-governmental organisations to engage more directly with the state. This kind of unmediated engagement may well be more adversarial than it has been in recent years, but this is surely a foreseeable consequence of the abandonment by the state of even a weak partnership approach to human rights and equality. This shameless attack on statutory bodies, or 'quangocide', may offend human rights activists, but it is no crime against humanity. Rather, it provides something of a reality check for those of us who might have been too believing about the post activist phase of human rights promotion and the capacity to achieve change through a close alignment with the state.

Taking human rights seriously is not the same thing as buying into a total manifesto for goodness and happy outcomes. Rather, it provides a way of engaging with profoundly complex and difficult questions in a manner that balances individual and wider societal interests. By overemphasising the degree to which human rights has all the answers – whether grounded in the natural law, positivist or other rights traditions – we run the real risk of damaging the very thing we set out to defend.

The 1948 Universal Declaration of Human Rights contains all the awkward questions that still need to be raised. While being stated at a necessary level of generality, its various articles do not supply detailed answers to those questions. The declaration does, however, provide an irreducible minimum, or moral bottom line, for the world, and the value system that it represents has spawned other important instruments, the legal value of which is more palpable. This is good enough reason to keep hope alive, even in a context in which despair is so readily an option.

DONNCHA O'CONNELL
Editor
December 2008

ALL HUMAN BEINGS ARE BORN FREE AND EQUAL IN DIGNITY AND RIGHTS. THEY ARE ENDOWED WITH REASON AND CONSCIENCE AND SHOULD ACT TOWARDS ONE ANOTHER IN A SPIRIT OF BROTHERHOOD.

ARTICLE 1

Colm O'Gorman

Executive Director of Amnesty International Ireland

In our work with other organisations in Ireland advocating for human rights like housing and health, we are often asked whether the fact that such rights exist in international law is of any use to people living in Ireland, given that those rights don't exist under Irish law. While our response is that international law is the standard to which the Irish government should be held accountable, the gap between what the government signs up to on our behalf and what they then incorporate into domestic law is glaring.

Amnesty International believes in the power of naming that which is clearly enshrined in international human rights law as a human rights issue and applying the standards set out in the UN system to the debate. Our work in the area of mental health is a clear example of the impact this can have. Increasingly, mental health is being cited in public discourse and in the media as a human rights issue. We see people who use mental health services articulating their rights, and we are seeing a growing capacity in the NGOs that campaign on mental health issues to draw down the international standards and apply them to the situation in Ireland.

Yet there remains a large gap between what government signs up to and what eventually becomes domestic law, particularly when it comes to economic, social and cultural rights. International law is very clear on the issue. There is a duty to incorporate human rights treaties ratified by Ireland. It is set out in the Charter of the United Nations and reiterated both in the convention on the law of treaties and in individual conventions. For example, the International Covenant on Civil and Political Rights specifically states that:

> Each State Party to the present Covenant under-takes to take the necessary steps, in accordance with its constitutional processes and with the provisions of the present Covenant, to adopt such laws or other measures as may be necessary to give effect to the rights recognized in the present Covenant.

So, from the inception of the UN, and right through each of the legal documents that have sprung from and expanded on the rights espoused in the Universal Declaration of Human Rights, it has been recognised that these rights, to be meaningful, must have domestic application.

Ireland is a 'dualist' state. This means that the international treaties which Ireland has ratified do not become part of domestic law unless the Oireachtas so determines. Thus, when Ireland signs and ratifies an international human rights treaty, the rights contained in it are not directly applicable to the people within the state as a matter of domestic law unless the Oireachtas passes legislation to incorporate the provisions of the treaty into domestic law or the Constitution is amended to give constitutional status to those provisions. By contrast, in 'monist' states, individuals derive rights directly from international law, which must be applied by national courts and have priority over any competing national law.

Dualism is a constitutional value typical of common law countries and is set out in Article 29 of Bunreacht na hÉireann 1937:

> No international agreements shall be part of the domestic law of the State save as may be determined by the Oireachtas.

Dualism, as a way of engaging with the international legal system, is founded on ostensibly good principles. Its intent is to safeguard the democratic legislative process by ensuring that the laws and rights of the people are not altered without the consent of their duly elected representatives. Typically, dualist states are not permitted to ratify international instruments unless their domestic laws already measure up to the minimum standards established by that instrument, although that assessment can, inevitably, be influenced by political as well as strictly legal considerations.

So, while our government may sign and ratify an international covenant, it has *no direct legal effect* in our municipal law, apart from any persuasive value it may have before the domestic courts.

Both Amnesty International and the government would agree that, within this debate, there are distortions of democracy. We don't, however, agree about where those distortions come from.

In defending the non-incorporation of the International Covenant on Economic, Social and Cultural Rights (ICESCR) to the UN, the civil servants who represented the government in 2002 argued that the insertion of ESC rights into the Irish Constitution would constitute a 'distortion of democracy', as policies in these areas should emerge through the democratic process, that is, through the will of the electorate as articulated and developed through political processes. They also argued that judicial rulings on ESC rights would interfere with the proper responsibility of government to set economic and social priorities within available resources.

Amnesty International would argue that the distortion lies elsewhere. Having a dualist system whereby international law must be 'incorporated' in order to be effective domestically is un-objectionable, if that is actually what happens. However, the vast majority of Ireland's international human rights obligations as set out in ratified treaties and covenants have not been incorporated directly or by reference into domestic law. Taking the European

Convention on Human Rights (ECHR) as an example, while the government ratified it in 1953, having been among the first ten countries to sign it in 1950, the convention was not incorporated (in a manner of speaking) into domestic law for almost fifty years, and then as a result of commitments made in the Good Friday Agreement of 1998. The government chose to give the convention 'interpretative' effect at a sub-constitutional level rather than direct statutory effect, thus minimising the potential impact of incorporation, which may, admittedly, have been slightly overstated given the substantial congruity between the rights protected by the Irish Constitution and the rights set forth in the convention.

Interestingly, the government has incorporated human rights treaties where the potential beneficiaries are outside the state. For example, the UN Convention against Torture is domestically enshrined through the Criminal Justice (United Nations Convention against Torture) Act 2000.

Thus government signs and ratifies international treaties on our behalf, but rarely incorporates them into domestic law. Arguably, the legislature could introduce bills to make real our human rights commitments, but in reality it does not have meaningful powers to initiate, debate, scrutinise and alter laws. Government policy objectives invariably hold sway in the legislative process.

There is a further distortion in relation to the democratic will of the people. Our government currently argues that enumerated rights can only emerge through the democratic process, i.e. if enough people want a particular right to be enshrined in the Constitution or in legislation, they will elect a party which will, if in government, make that happen. However, the government is prepared to sign up to international covenants with no process for meaningful public debate. The majority of people have little or no idea what is and is not being signed up to in their name on the international front. And for those most in need of protection, like members of the Traveller community or immigrants, the rights they have under international law may never emerge through the democratic process, which, by its nature, does not necessarily respond to minorities.

The failure to provide adequate human rights education is also problematic. How can people access rights if they are unaware what their rights are? Many people have little idea about what their human rights are and are thus in a weak position to make their voices heard through the 'democratic system'. The day we see constituents turning up at TDs' clinics expressing concern at the government's silence during the negotiation of Optional Protocol to the ICESCR or its failure to sign the Migrant Worker's Convention is a long way off indeed.

The Irish government frequently points to the 1937 Constitution as more than adequately fulfilling its substantive international obligations in the domestic sphere. The UN repeatedly advises the government that this is simply not sufficient. Experience in recent years shows how, even where rights are enshrined in the Constitution, official resistance towards the vindication of those rights can be strong. In February 2008, it was revealed that over the past decade, the Department of Education had spent €5 million fighting parents of children with autism in the courts, money that surely might have been better spent on actually providing services for those children.

Incomplete incorporation of international human rights commitments is not a legal or constitutional problem, but one of *political will*. Therefore, unless legislative incorporation becomes a more routine part of how government engages with the international legal system, dualism, Irish-style, remains inherently hypocritical. Ireland's record on incorporation diminishes the value of our commitments under the Universal Declaration of Human Rights and undermines our global moral authority as a leading proponent of human rights.

If the human rights that the Irish government signs up to on our behalf are to have any meaningful impact on the lives of people living in this country, fresh thinking is needed. At the very least, we should have stronger Oireachtas involvement in the treaty-making processes and in Ireland's decisions regarding the signing and ratification of such treaties. Civil society groups must be allowed to play a role in influencing government policy objectives to be furthered through legislation. The role of the Irish Human Rights Commission, which is uniquely placed to offer guidance to government on the application of human rights standards, must be protected through the provision of adequate resources.

There is wonderful resonance between the 1916 Proclamation of the Irish Republic and the 1948 Universal Declaration of Human Rights. Both clearly envisage a new world order where the inherent rights and dignity of each individual are protected and celebrated. It seems that Ireland, as represented by successive governments, is a country strong on rhetoric but weak on the realisation of those rights.

EVERYONE IS ENTITLED TO ALL THE RIGHTS AND
FREEDOMS SET FORTH IN THIS DECLARATION, WITHOUT
DISTINCTION OF ANY KIND, SUCH AS RACE, COLOUR, SEX,
LANGUAGE, RELIGION, POLITICAL OR OTHER OPINION,
NATIONAL OR SOCIAL ORIGIN, PROPERTY, BIRTH OR
OTHER STATUS. FURTHERMORE, NO DISTINCTION SHALL
BE MADE ON THE BASIS OF POLITICAL, JURISDICTIONAL
OR INTERNATIONAL STATUS OF THE COUNTRY OR
TERRITORY TO WHICH A PERSON BELONGS, WHETHER IT
BE INDEPENDENT, TRUST, NON-SELF-GOVERNING OR
UNDER ANY OTHER LIMITATION OF SOVEREIGNTY.

ARTICLE 2

Niall Crowley

Former CEO of the Equality Authority

**Introduction: An Equality Infrastructure to Match the Universal
Declaration of Human Rights**

Article 2 places equality and non-discrimination at the heart of the
Universal Declaration of Human Rights. It is appropriate, as we mark

the declaration's sixtieth anniversary, to briefly assess the institutional and legal infrastructure established in Ireland to promote equality and combat discrimination. Does this infrastructure match the commitment to equality and non-discrimination established in the Universal Declaration of Human Rights? Is it adequate to meet the challenge posed by the level and nature of discrimination and inequality experienced in Irish society?

Infrastructure

A significant infrastructure to promote equality of opportunity and to combat discrimination has been developed in Ireland. The Employment Equality Acts 1998–2004 prohibit discrimination in the workplace and in vocational training. The Equal Status Acts 2000–2004 prohibit discrimination in the provision of goods and services, accommodation and education. These acts cover the nine grounds of gender, marital status, family status, age, disability, sexual orientation, race, religion and membership of the Traveller community.

Two separate institutions were established under the equality legislation. The Equality Authority has a statutory mandate to promote equality of opportunity and to combat discrimination in the areas covered by the equality legislation. The Equality Tribunal is a quasi-judicial body established to mediate cases taken under equality legislation or to investigate such cases, hearing all persons interested and desiring to be heard, issuing decisions and providing for redress.

The equality legislation includes some provisions that acknowledge the importance of a positive recognition of difference in combating discrimination and promoting equality. This would appear, valuably, to go beyond the formula of 'without distinction of any kind' used in the Universal Declaration of Human Rights. Equality can only be achieved through recognition of difference rather than through the pursuit of sameness.

Equality legislation requires reasonable accommodation of people with disabilities. Employers are required to make adjustments for employees and prospective employees with disabilities, provided this does not cause a disproportionate burden. Service providers are required to provide special treatment or special facilities for customers with disabilities, provided this does not cost more than a nominal cost. It is of note that, in 2006 and 2007, the disability ground constituted the highest area of case files of the Equality Authority under equality legislation, with the majority of cases involving a failure by employers and service providers to make reasonable accommodation for people with disabilities.

The Equality Authority has recommended that these reasonable accommodation provisions should be explicitly required across all nine grounds covered in the legislation. A case supported by the Equality Authority (*Rasaq vs. Campbell Catering,* Labour Court EED 048) under the Employment Equality Acts and heard by the Labour Court has resulted in an interpretation of the equality legislation that extends this approach to the race ground. The Labour Court clarified that discrimination can occur not only where two people are treated differently despite their circumstances being the same, but also where two people are treated the same despite their circumstances being different. In the particular case, cultural and linguistic difference created a context where the circumstances of individual workers were different when it came to applying disciplinary procedures. If adjustments are not made to take account of such differences, discrimination can occur.

Limitations

However, significant limitations to the equality legislation mean that it fails to match the commitment evident in Article 2 of the Universal Declaration of Human Rights.

One such limitation relates to the grounds covered by the equality legislation. When the legislation was enacted in the late 1990s, it marked a significant expansion in scope of application with its coverage of nine grounds. Previous equality legislation was confined to the grounds of gender and marital status. The experience of implementing the equality legislation since it came into force in 1999 has clarified the need to expand these grounds further. The Equality Authority has already recommended the introduction of an additional four grounds – socio-economic status, political opinion, trade union membership and criminal conviction. There has been no positive response from the government to this recommendation – yet even this recommendation falls short of the comprehensive approach in the Universal Declaration of Human Rights, which names eleven grounds and includes – to address the issue of a non-exhaustive list of possible instances of discrimination – any 'other status'.

Another limitation relates to the scope of the Equal Status Acts. The Equal Status Acts do not explicitly cover the functions of the state – functions such as immigration control and policing in particular. This too falls short of the approach of the Universal Declaration of Human Rights.

In its submission, *Embedding Equality in Immigration Policy*, the Equality Authority recommended that immigration legislation, policies and procedures should adhere to the substantive principle of equality. This recommendation reflected that, in immigration, the state is making a process available to the migrant and the migrant submits to this process and to the application of standards to his or her case. In such a context, the state needs to bind itself to ensuring the process adheres to the substantive principle of equality. This requires, at a minimum, that the definition of services under the Equal Status Acts should be expanded to explicitly include the functions of the state to bring immigration control and police powers within the ambit of the Equal Status Acts.

A further limitation relates to the broad statutory exemption in the Equal Status Acts. Section 14 exempts from the application of the Equal Status Acts action required by other legislation. In effect, this allows the state to legislate to discriminate by means of statutory override. Again, this provision falls short of the ideals of the Universal Declaration of Human Rights.

This exemption was used when the Department of Social and Family Affairs introduced an amendment under the Social Welfare (Miscellaneous) Provisions Act 2004 to limit the definition of 'spouse' and 'couple' to married couples and to cohabiting couples of the opposite sex. This amendment overturned a settlement in respect of a same-sex couple agreed in a case supported by the Equality Authority. It enables the department to discriminate against same-sex couples in relation to a range of non-statutory administrative schemes, such as the free travel scheme which was the focus of the settled case.

Adequacy

For rights to be effectively guaranteed and fully realised, there must be effective enforcement mechanisms. It is therefore important to assess the adequacy of the equality infrastructure established by law to respond effectively to the level and nature of discrimination being experienced in Ireland. Research carried out by the Economic and Social Research Institute (ESRI), *The Experience of Discrimination in Ireland*, puts this issue of adequacy in a particularly challenging context.

This research highlighted that 12.5 per cent (over 380,000 people) of the population aged eighteen years and over had experienced discrimination in the preceding two years on the nine grounds covered by the equality legislation, as well as on other grounds. The scale of discrimination reported goes beyond the capacity of the current equality infrastructure. The research found that groups reporting the highest level of discrimination were the least likely to take action on foot of this experience – only 6 per cent of those who reported discrimination were found to have taken any formal action in response to this experience.

The capacity of the institutions established under the equality legislation is already overstretched. The Equality Authority has highlighted significant delays in the appointment of equality officers, scheduling of hearings and delivery of recommendations by the Equality Tribunal. The social partners secured an important commitment in the national social partnership agreement, *Towards 2016*, to review expenditure on the equality infrastructure and highlighted the removal of the backlog of cases before the Equal Tribunal as a particular priority. During 2008, improvements were noted in relation to these delays, but this is still in a context where only 6 per cent of those reporting discrimination take any formal action in response.

The ESRI research raises serious questions about the adequacy of the equality infrastructure in place to respond to the levels of discrimination reported. In this regard, the disproportionate reduction of 43 per cent in the Equality Authority budget must be viewed with deep concern. The Equality Authority has already indicated that this may render it unable to fully or effectively carry out the full range of its core functions. The very viability of the organisation is threatened.

A proactive approach to preventing discrimination is also particularly important in a context where people clearly face significant barriers in responding effectively to experiences of discrimination. Recent work on human rights has made cogent arguments that 'a conception of human rights [is needed] which gives rise, not just to a duty of restraint on the State, but also to a series of positive duties on the State' (Fredman, *Human Rights Transformed*, Oxford University Press, 2008).

Irish equality legislation lags behind similar legislation in Northern Ireland and in Britain, where there is a positive duty on the public sector to have due regard to equality in carrying out their functions. The Equality Authority has recommended the inclusion of similar provisions in Irish equality legislation, which would be important in securing action that would prevent discrimination in the public sector. This positive duty would enhance the adequacy of the equality legislation, particularly in a context where, in 2007, 69 per cent of all Equality Authority case files under the Equal Status Acts involved allegations of discrimination against public-sector bodies.

This issue of adequacy raises significant challenges in relation to a capacity to give full and proper effect to the ideals of Article 2 of the Universal Declaration of Human Rights in Ireland. It will be important to sustain a focus on this issue and to seek necessary change as we mark the sixtieth anniversary of the UDHR.

EVERYONE HAS THE RIGHT TO LIFE, LIBERTY AND SECURITY OF PERSON.

ARTICLE 3

Lieutenant General Dermot Earley

Chief of Staff of the Irish Defence Forces

Life, Liberty and Security of Person: A Soldier's View

Article 3 of the Universal Declaration of Human Rights brings together and guarantees three key rights. The full text of the article reads simply: 'Everyone has the right to life, liberty and security of person.' The articulation is elegant, comprehensive and irrefutable. However, it is not self-explanatory and so later work by the UN necessarily expanded on and exemplified the principles this and the twenty-nine other articles of the UDHR are based on.

This work includes the International Covenant on Civil and Political Rights 1966, which prohibits 'arbitrary arrest or detention' and goes on to stipulate that: 'No one shall be deprived of his liberty except on such grounds and in accordance with such procedure as are established by law' (Article 9(1)). The significance of Article 3 of the UDHR is best reflected in the fact that it has been incorporated verbatim into the constitutions of countries as far apart as Germany, Japan, Canada and, most recently, South Africa. Indeed, as Amnesty International has noted, it has become a staple of many subsequent human rights standards and statements.

The right to life is universally accepted as the most fundamental basic human right. Ireland fully supports this principle and we can be particularly proud that it is explicitly enshrined in the 1937 Constitution, which every individual member of the Defence Forces takes an oath to defend. All other human rights cascade from this basic human right, as do arguments for pluralism and tolerance. As a people, we are increasingly global in our perspectives and our concerns. Perhaps this is one of the reasons why in more prosperous times Ireland was one of the few countries in the world to contribute €200 per capita in foreign aid via Irish Aid, making it the sixth-largest aid donor in the world in terms of GNP.

This global vision is certainly a factor in the idealism of Ireland's youth who continue to volunteer to work in developing countries through excellent organisations such as Concern, GOAL, Trócaire and Amnesty International, to mention but a few. And it also plays a part, arguably, in why so many Irish people work with the United Nations (UN), including the UN headquarters in New York, the World Health Organization, World Food Programme and the UN High Commissioner for Refugees. The latter office alone has assisted an estimated 50 million people over the last five decades. We in the defence forces contribute in a very practical manner to this project by pre-positioning emergency supplies in our training centre in the Curragh on behalf of Irish Aid and by providing training to the recently established Rapid Response Corps through the United Nations Training School Ireland, a component of our Military College.

Similarly, the Irish Defence Forces has to date contributed to 74 UN-mandated overseas peacekeeping missions, consisting of almost 60,000 individual tours of duty. Eighty-five Irish soldiers have lost their lives in the service of peace overseas, a number of whom I am proud to have known and served with. It is to the challenge of honouring Article 3 of the UDHR within a military life that I now wish to turn.

Those in the Irish Defence Forces reflect the times and the wider community they live in and so take pride in the contribution Ireland makes to world peace and security through the medium of peace support and crisis management operations. The Defence Forces is relatively small but operate well above what mere numbers might indicate.

Members of our defence forces are recognised worldwide for their professionalism, quality and leadership. To achieve high standards, we train and prepare our personnel for Peace Support Operations in a manner rooted distinctly in UN doctrine and practices. Increasingly, we are mindful of culture, gender and heritage and civil–military co-operation (CIMIC) is an integral component of this process. We seek to develop military practices that integrate more efficiently and effectively within comprehensive arrangements for multidimensional and increasingly complex UN-mandated missions where military, UN agencies, UN police and other inter-national agencies work together to create and maintain peace. To further this, overseas experience and conceptual peacekeeping studies are integrated in the Centre of Excellence in Human Rights and Law of Armed Conflict, established in the United Nations Training School Ireland in the Military College. Most importantly, Irish peacekeepers seek to fulfil, in a very true sense, the principles articulated in Article 3 of the UDHR.

Irish involvement in Peace Support Operations is premised on a UN mandate normally given under Chapter 6 or Chapter 7 of the UN Charter. We place central importance on being a member of the UN, which carries considerable moral authority and emphasises humanitarian interest in its approach to international crises. Any use of force must, first and foremost, be legitimate in accordance with international law, proportionate and impartial. This is particularly important when we send Irish troops into troubled places as witnesses to events and aspects of human nature that can shock and appal. It is crucial to us as soldiers that we never lose sight of Article 3 of the Universal Declaration. It serves as our guide to judgement and our personal touchstone. A deep understanding of Article 3 facilitates the essential measured approach to Peace Support Operations from the force commander to the peacekeeper on the ground. Each Irish soldier on overseas service carries a card that states: 'Defence Forces personnel engaged on peace support operations have international obligations under the United Nations Charter, the Universal Declaration of Human Rights and the European Convention on Human Rights to act to prevent violations of human rights, to react against violations of human rights and to act to rebuild human rights when violated.'

The United Nations has seen many changes and challenges since its establishment on 24 October 1945. From the outset, it has been a place where traditions have met – the late nineteenth- to early twentieth-century traditions of great power and of universalism in particular. It is a project that has always had its critics as well as its passionate advocates, but there can be no doubting the central role that the UN has played in international affairs since its inception. Justice for individuals has come to be accepted as a concomitant of international peace and order largely because of the efforts of the UN organisation and its various organs and commissions.

It is important to view the origins and the framing of the Universal Declaration of Human Rights in this context. When, in 1947, a UN delegation chaired by Eleanor Roosevelt was tasked with drafting what was described in 2002 by Glendon as 'the world's first standard statement of human rights', they took up a challenge that seemed 'both impossible and supremely necessary'. That we are now celebrating the sixtieth anniversary of the document they produced is testament to the success they made of that task.

Soldiers, as participants in Peace Support Operations, must deal with broken societies, lawlessness and a negation of human rights on a scale that is almost incomprehensible to those who have not experienced it. The 'right to life, liberty and security of person' is taken for granted on this island – others are less fortunate. Irish Defence Forces personnel deployed on a UN-mandated mission are bound to uphold both the highest ethical and moral standards in accordance with the UDHR. Article 3 may be a statement of an ideal best appreciated when read alongside the other twenty-nine articles of the declaration. Ideals are necessarily aspirational, particularly when they manifest themselves as a desire to uphold human rights in all their forms and in every way possible. The relevance of this to Ireland in 2009 and the influence it has in our beliefs and value systems reaches far beyond our shores: the men and women of the Irish Defence Forces – and indeed those who seek out roles in UN and NGO activities take it with them when they go out in the service of peace.

NO ONE SHALL BE HELD IN SLAVERY OR SERVITUDE; SLAVERY AND THE SLAVE TRADE SHALL BE PROHIBITED IN ALL THEIR FORMS.

ARTICLE 4

Kathleen Fahy

Ruhama

Our concept of slavery has been shaped by the experience and images of the transatlantic slave trade, which saw the mass forced transportation of millions of West African men and women to the Americas to toil in the tobacco and cotton plantations. This phenomenon, which began in the fifteenth century and lasted for nearly four hundred years, was declared illegitimate in 1807. Our collective image of that pernicious activity is of Africans being herded onto overcrowded ships, frequently in shackles and, following a long and arduous voyage, being sold in open markets to the highest bidder. While slavery has been in existence since history was recorded, this particular manifestation of it has to date been the most organised enslavement of peoples known to us and has informed our opinion on this massive and structured abuse of humans. We have not yet generally accommodated our thinking to the newer forms of enslavement which are currently taking place.

There is a tendency, therefore, towards optimism that slavery is something which has been consigned to history or, perhaps, exists on a small scale in cultural and economic contexts far removed from our own. We might not be so sanguine if we realised that slavery has adapted different guises, different names to disguise the practice – 'bonded labour', 'sweatshops', 'human trafficking', 'sex tourism' – names that as yet do not evoke the emotional undertones of the word 'slavery' and so give inadequate expression to the human abuse at their core. 'Victims' in areas like 'sex tourism' are reduced to mere factors of monetary value and, as such, are denied their humanity and intrinsic worth. This is enslavement.

Ruhama works with victims of commercial sexual exploitation and I propose to focus on the relevance of Article 4 of the Universal Declaration of Human Rights to one particular group, i.e. women in prostitution and women trafficked into the commercial sex trade.

Trafficking for Sexual Exploitation Today

The crude recruitment methods of previous centuries do not apply today. Instead of press gangs, more duplicitous and covert tactics are employed. Potential victims (predominantly young people) are targeted, befriended, offered a job or study opportunity abroad or deceived into a relationship which promises far more than the trafficker intends to deliver. In their desire to escape from a certain future of continued poverty and deprivation and to build a better life elsewhere, victims naively collude in the process, acquiescing in the use of false identities and documentation to facilitate travel and entry to the destination country.

On arrival, the bright future promised to these women quickly evaporates as the truth emerges. Enormous debts have supposedly been incurred in organising their documentation and passage and these must be repaid. There is no other job on offer except prostitution. Their illegal status, their falsified papers, the illegality of their situation all now make them vulnerable to the trafficker or his accomplices, who may be the only people they actually know in the new country. If they still refuse to co-operate, rape, physical violence and threats against family back home are all used to achieve compliance.

Long working hours, meeting up to ten 'clients' a day, restricted movement and minimal contact with the outside world becomes the norm, all a long way from the dream of prosperity which made them vulnerable to the predatory attentions of the trafficker in the first instance.

There is no doubt that human trafficking is the modern face of slavery. The defining conditions of coercion and control, involuntary servitude or forced labour, as the person becomes someone else's property, are all apparent. The slave merchants who ferried slaves across the Atlantic did so because they knew there were willing buyers on the other side who would make their efforts worthwhile. So, today, the modern trafficker operates with the assurance of a ready market and handsome profits. The market, which so many people participate in, drives this abuse.

Any form of slavery is degrading, but there is an additional oppression and stigma for victims of sex trafficking. Not only are their rights infringed through the exploitative conditions and coercive circumstances they find themselves in, they are also trapped in an activity which, of itself, is a violation of their human rights and bodily integrity. Nonetheless, there has been an unprecedented growth in the global sex industry in recent years and a massive increase in the number of women and children being trafficked to respond to growing demand.

Consider this – 12 million Africans were enslaved between the fifteenth and nineteenth centuries, when slavery was an accepted and legal practice. In the opening decade of the twenty-first century, it is estimated that between 600,000 and 800,000 people are trafficked across international borders annually. If even the lowest of these annual estimates is allowed to continue, modern-day human trafficking is set to overtake the transatlantic slave trade in less than two decades. Moreover, 70 per cent of people trafficked today are women and children and 80 per cent of these are trafficked into the sex trade, predominantly in Europe, North America and Asia. This is a global phenomenon. In contrast to former times, Ireland is firmly enmeshed in this contemporary round of slavery.

With such a high proportion of trafficked victims ending up in prostitution or some other area of the sex trade, any discussion of modern slavery has to address the issue of prostitution and the role it plays in the enslavement of millions of women and children throughout the world.

The Failure of Human Rights to Address Prostitution

It is indeed a strange irony that over recent decades, in which we have successfully drawn on established human rights instruments to help redress oppression and create positive normative standards in so many areas, the issue of prostitution has not only escaped inclusion as a form of slavery but has, in some countries, been legalised in the name of human rights. The right to self-determination (in this case, the right of a woman to engage in consensual sex for a price) and the right to work (prostitution being no different from other forms of work and, as such, requiring regulation like any other profession) are key arguments put forward by the pro-prostitution lobby. This viewpoint assumes free agency, equality in the encounter and that the woman selling her body has the power to effect a fair outcome from the transaction.

In the name of freedom to choose, we accept prostitution, but it is difficult to see real choice – other than that of the 'consumer' – being exercised in these situations. The experience of Ruhama is that, in the vast majority of cases, the above assumptions do not hold. Where is the self-determination when a woman is in prostitution to feed a drug habit or is being pimped by a partner? Where is the free choice when the range of options open to a young woman is so limited that prostitution seems the only possibility? Is power not firmly weighted in favour of the buyer when the street worker's immediate need for cash forces her to lower her price or engage unwillingly in specific sexual activities? It is difficult to see equality in these exchanges.

For Ruhama, the human right to be considered here is the right *not* to be prostituted; the right to be able to earn one's living with dignity, free from exploitation and valued as a person, not as a commodity to be bought and sold. To draw distinctions between trafficking and prostitution – seeing one as forced and ob-jectionable and the other as voluntary and acceptable – is meaningless. But this distinction allows us to accommodate the abuse that is prostitution while we decry the means used to procure a steady supply of women to meet the demands of the prostitution trade. Moreover, it must surely render ineffective all our efforts to combat trafficking, as only the procurement process is criminalised and not the resultant abuse itself.

In 1949, the UN was quite clear that organised prostitution was the economic and structural foundation of sex trafficking. It noted that: 'Prostitution and the accompanying evil of the traffic in persons for the purpose of prostitution are incompatible with the dignity and worth of the human person and endanger the welfare of the individual.' Again, in 2000, the *UN Protocol to Prevent, Suppress and Punish Trafficking in Persons* stated, categorically, that 'exploitation shall include, at a minimum, the exploitation of the prostitution of others, or other forms of sexual exploitation'. As a community of states, we have made the linkage between prostitution and slavery. We have made the declarations but we now need to take action, otherwise Article 4 of the UDHR, which provides that no one shall be held in slavery or servitude, will continue to remain an aspiration and the shameful exploitation of hundreds of thousands of women and children will continue.

Transatlantic slavery was finally abolished when it became morally unacceptable to people who were prepared to act to bring about its end. There was, of course, resistance from those who benefited and profited from its pursuit. Eventually, it was appreciated that slavery was as dehumanising for the society that tolerated it as it was for its victims. Just as we now abhor the concept of slavery, perhaps future generations will look back and wonder why we failed for so long to recognise that the current trade in human flesh is just as dehumanising and damaging as were the shackles of earlier forms of slavery. They might also wonder why we were blind for so long to the human rights violations involved.

NO ONE SHALL BE SUBJECTED TO TORTURE OR TO CRUEL, INHUMAN OR DEGRADING TREATMENT OR PUNISHMENT.

ARTICLE 5

Margaret Martin

Director of Women's Aid

Think of someone being handcuffed, burned with cigarettes, kicked in the head and stomach, with clothing tied over their head, and beaten. Think of them being choked until unconscious, threatened with firearms, a gun held to the head, tied up and locked in a room for days without food. What picture emerges?

More than likely you will picture a man, a political prisoner, in some foreign, distant land. But these abuses are not from some faraway land. They happened here in Ireland, not to political prisoners but to women – women who were often prisoners in their own homes, women living with an abusive partner. They are a small sample of the cruel and inhuman treatment disclosed to Women's

Aid Helpline in 2007. Sadly, these snapshots have not differed significantly over the thirty years that Women's Aid has been hearing women's experiences of domestic violence.

The connections between domestic violence and Article 5 of the Universal Declaration of Human Rights may not seem obvious at first. Torture, cruel, inhuman or degrading treatment or punishment all have legal definitions under the UN Convention against Torture 1984. These include a number of essential factors involving intentional exposure to significant mental or physical pain or suffering by or with the consent or acquiescence of the state authorities.

Leaving aside the role of the state – and it does have a role in the area of prevention and protection – let us consider both the issues of intention and the exposure to mental or physical pain and suffering to get a deeper understanding of the qualitative connections between Article 5 of the UDHR and domestic violence.

Intention

According to Bunch and Carrillo (Attic Press, 1992):

> Victims are chosen because of their gender. The message is domination: stay in your place or be afraid. Contrary to the argument that such violence is only personal or cultural, it is profoundly political. It results from the structural relationships of power, domination and privilege between men and women in society. Violence against women is central to maintaining those political relations at home, at work and in all public spheres.

One of the most common forms of violence against women internationally is domestic violence. What makes domestic violence unique is the intimate relationship that exists between the abuser and abused. The majority of abuse disclosed to the Women's Aid National Freephone Helpline in 2007 was perpetrated by a current male intimate partner. Within such intimate relationships, the abusive partner has constant access to his victim as well as a safe, private space in which to carry out the abuse. The nature of the relationship also means that he has detailed, indeed intimate, knowledge about the most effective ways to abuse his victim.

Contrary to myth, domestic violence is not a series of isolated incidents, unconnected and disparate, related to alcohol, anger or loss of control. Rather, domestic violence is an intentional and, usually, relentless pattern of abusive behaviours designed to instil fear in order to maintain power and control. Often, the abuse begins in a small way, gradually becoming more severe until the woman finds herself living in fear, unable to sleep, terrified to leave, a prisoner in her own home. In many cases, severe abuse becomes unnecessary over time as the threat or anticipation of abuse suffices to control her.

As with torture and other forms of cruel, degrading and inhuman treatment or punishment, the abuser's motivation is control through fear. The consequences can be devastating. The Centre for the Care of Survivors of Torture describes the aim of torture as being to destroy the identity of the individual, to humiliate, weaken and destroy their personality. The recognition of rape as a weapon of war acknowledges that the intent behind rape is to subjugate and humiliate in this way. In 2002, the SAVI report (Sexual Abuse and Violence in Ireland) revealed that almost one-quarter of perpetrators of sexual violence were intimate partners or former partners.

In 1990, marital rape was criminalised in Ireland, but since then, there has been only one successful conviction. Women's Aid is very aware of how common this form of abuse is and of how deep feelings of shame and embarrassment make it one of the most difficult forms of domestic abuse to disclose. Those disclosures that we have heard regularly include forced re-enactment of pornography, rape including gang rape, being urinated on following rape and being raped with implements.

Significant Mental or Physical Pain and Suffering

> I had three children and two miscarriages. From the first beating to the last beating; from the first time he stole a life; from the first time he raped me, it affected me very badly. One night he held me down and raped me. I shouted at him to stop. He used me like a rag doll and he hit me when I moved. It went on for hours. When I thought it was over he said, 'You can sleep now, you bitch.' I tried to get up from the bed and he pulled me down again and anally raped me. He pushed a pillow onto my face so he wouldn't hear me shout. I felt like a prisoner to him.

> Amy's story from *Living to Tell the Tale*
> (Domestic Violence Response Ltd, 2004)

The tactics used by domestic violence perpetrators share many commonalities with the tactics used by those engaged in torture and other forms of cruel, degrading and inhuman treatment or punishment. Domestic violence includes a myriad of abuses, from physical to sexual and emotional, all of which can have devastating and long-term impacts on the victim.

Every day on the Women's Aid Helpline, we listen to women's experiences of abuse. Physical abuse is often minimised and thought of as just a push or shove, but it can reach levels of real severity. This violence frequently results in physical injury, often serious, and sometimes may even result in death. Of the 146 female homicides in Ireland since 1996, 50 per cent of the resolved cases were committed by a husband, ex-husband, partner or ex-partner. Of these, 18 per cent of women were beaten to death, 28 per cent were strangled and 31 per cent were stabbed to death.

While often less well understood, emotional abuse can be just as damaging, breaking down a woman's spirit and eroding her confidence and sense of self-esteem. Disclosures to Women's Aid include:

- being humiliated and denied privacy, not being allowed to go to the toilet alone, abuser accompanying her to the GP or hospital;
- sleep deprivation, being constantly woken, threats to rape while sleeping, waking to find the abuser with a weapon in his hands;
- not being allowed to speak without permission, destroying personal and sentimental belongings, threatening to kill her and/or their children;

- never being called by her own name, constantly being called names, such as 'stupid', 'ugly', 'bitch'; and
- being isolated from family and friends, not being allowed to go out alone, keeping track of petrol to track her movements.

As with the impact of torture and cruel, inhuman or degrading treatment or punishment, the impact of domestic violence on women can be devastating and lifelong and includes: death; injuries and hospitalisation; feeling trapped and powerless; depression and suicidal feelings; complete physical and emotional isolation from family and friends; feelings of shame and embarrassment; long-term anxiety; an inability to communicate with others; and general ill-health. These parallels with torture and its impact were illustrated in a *Guardian* article of 13 March 2004 which stated, in the words of a detainee: 'The whole point of Guantánamo was to get to you psychologically. The beatings were not nearly as bad as the psychological torture – bruises heal after a week, but the other stuff stays with you.'

Prevalence of Domestic Violence

Domestic violence occurs in every social and economic grouping of society, in all ethnic groups and cultures and among people of every educational and geographical background. There is no 'type' of woman it occurs to and there is no 'type' of home it happens in. The risk factor is being female. According to Kimmel (2001), 90 per cent of the more systematic, persistent and injurious violence that is instrumental in the maintenance of power is perpetrated by men.

In a study commissioned by Women's Aid in 1995, it was revealed that domestic violence is a very real threat to women in Ireland, as it affects one in five women. The Women's Aid National Freephone Helpline consistently responds to around 12,000 calls annually. In 2007, there were 8,012 incidents of emotional abuse, 2,457 incidents of physical abuse and 593 incidents of sexual abuse, including 248 incidents of rape, disclosed by women calling the Helpline. Some of the most disturbing incidents related to abuse during pregnancy. It is quite shocking to read that, according to the Royal College of Midwives (1997), one-quarter of women experiencing domestic violence are assaulted for the first time during pregnancy and, according to a study by O'Donnell, Fitzpatrick and McKenna (2000), one in eight pregnant women attending the Rotunda Hospital in Dublin had experienced abuse from a partner while pregnant.

According to the National Network of Women's Refuges and Support Services, there were 1,952 women accommodated in refuges in Ireland in 2006. During the same year, 2,985 children also stayed in refuge. Refuge provision in Ireland remains inadequate and many women and children are denied access to refuge each year. For example, in 2004, the three refuges in the Eastern Region refused more than twice as many women as they accommodated.

Many women continue to experience domestic violence even after they have attempted to free themselves from the violence, with stalking, physical threats, phone/text harassment, damage to property and sexual assault being common ongoing abuses.

Conclusion

While the world in general condemns torture and other forms of cruel and inhuman treatment, the response to domestic violence is more ambivalent. What condemnation or sanctions do domestic violence abusers fear? Despite the introduction of the Domestic Violence Act 1996 and increased reporting levels to An Garda Síochána, the conviction rate has dropped from 16 per cent in 1997 to 6.5 per cent in 2002, according to a country report by the National Observatory on Violence Against Women (2004). In effect, the majority of abusers go free of penalty and public condemnation.

If this fundamental human right was being violated so consistently and pervasively in any other realm of Irish society, there would be public outrage and serious state action to protect the human rights of victims. The work currently underway by Cosc, the National Office for the Prevention of Domestic, Sexual and Gender-Based Violence, in developing its strategic plan is encouraging in this regard. As we mark the sixtieth anniversary of the Universal Declaration of Human Rights, it is time that we pay due attention with appropriate protections and support for those being abused in the private domestic sphere, underscored by effective sanctions for their abusers.

EVERYONE HAS THE RIGHT TO RECOGNITION EVERYWHERE AS A PERSON BEFORE THE LAW.

ARTICLE 6

Rosaleen McDonagh

Traveller

There were three of them – a medical doctor, a judge and another man in a suit. The room was clean and sparse, a light pink colour, two windows, a table with a bible in the middle. Jessica Ward sat between her barrister and solicitor at the other end of the table.

She went into the room and the three men stood up. This might be court etiquette, but she had been told that this was not a court. This hearing would be supportive, in so far as a hearing could be. Seeing men standing up made her feel intimidated. It reminded her of years of being talked down to and being talked at. Even as an adult woman, she was always conscious of people's height, regardless of context. These men were powerful. There was no need for them to show it.

Normally, Jessica Ward would get great joy using the riser in her electric wheelchair. Eye-to-eye contact was how she liked to look at the world. The chair was her secret weapon. Having non-disabled people look down or bend over her gave her no breath, no space and no room for her voice to travel and be heard. Today, her hands were rigid with nerves. The magic button on her chair felt too hard to push. Jessica was told she wasn't allowed to have any family member in the hearing with her, no personal assistant, nor any other female companion. She had an innate feeling or questioning inside herself. In a room filled with strangers, who will understand what I'm saying? It was going to be a long day, Jessica thought. None of them will be able to understand my cerebral palsy voice.

She was all dolled up. Jessica Ward had long dark hair. She wore gold jewellery, plenty of it on her fingers, her hands and her neck. It was borrowed from her sisters for the occasion. The big gold hoops in her ears hurt her when she turned sideways, but they were a prerequisite, not an accessory. She knew what look she wanted. Her clothes were modest but very stylish. Now she was glad she had decided not to wear a suit. The bright ethnic colours that she wore gave her confidence. Others had advised her to tone things down, but Jessica Ward had seen beyond settled snobbery. She ignored connotations about class and dress. The value of Traveller status for her was not tied to romanticism or folklore, it was more than an academic debate. She embodied Traveller ethnicity. She had paid the price for that embodiment. Ms Ward had Traveller chic down to a fine art. She would flaunt her Traveller identity, and even if these people pretended not to see it, she would shove it in their faces. It made her feel strong and proud, today of all days. It was her strongest reserve.

They only wanted to see her disability. That was all they could manage. Keep it clean. Moral boundaries would come into play. Jessica knew it was easy to have empathy for something that was visual. They had dealt with disabled people before her case. That history was recorded, believed, recognised. There was even an apology given by the state to disabled people. 'Travellers were ignored but we were there in those evil institutions,' Jessica had written in her statement. A hundred speeches were in her head, things that she had wanted to say for so long. I'm entitled to be a little indignant, even self-righteous, she thought. But sadness took over Jessica Ward's courage. Numbness left no room for ego or any attempt to talk.

No words would come out. Her plan was not to give in, not to let them break her. Crying was too easy. Yet the plans in Jessica's head never even got a chance to be tested. The men just focused on two parts of her allegations. In an effort to hold her memory and to pull herself out of emotional chaos, Jessica left the room a few times.

'They accept everything, you don't have to say any more,' the barrister said.

'What about my Traveller identity?' Jessica asked.

'Well, no, but everything else,' said the barrister.

'Nothing else matters!' was Jessica's reply.

There were too many notes, too many papers being shuffled round. Too many settled voices in her head and now they were telling her, we don't want to hear you talk! We don't want to hear the anger and pain in your voice, but mostly, as settled people, we don't believe you, or others like you, who claim that Traveller children were treated differently to other children. She blew her nose and said to her barrister and solicitor, 'I'm going back in there and I'm saying what I need to say.' They had their notes in front of them and were asking Ms Jessica Ward about dates. She said, 'I don't remember.' She said, 'You have the facts, I have my reality.'

They checked her again. Had she read her statement? Jessica was crying. She said, 'No.' The cross-examining was getting out of hand. Jessica felt it was a waste. To them, she was not a real Traveller, she was too clean, too smart. In their eyes, Jessica Ward was losing and she knew it. Her Traveller identity would not be taken into account. This confused her; ten minutes previously they had accepted everything. Records and dates had matched. This horrible history had been too hard to live with for years, let alone verbalise now. Her body was distressed. She knew her strong emotions were feeding their stereotype of her as being an unreasonable, angry Traveller woman.

The middle man asked Jessica, 'Ms Ward, are you making a political point?'

She answered, 'I have many other arenas to be on a political crusade. This is personal. It's private. I want the hurt to stop.'

The man continued to speak. 'Are you suggesting that your surname was an integral component of what you may have suffered?'

She nodded.

Then Jessica said, 'I don't expect any of you can understand. Being a Traveller in this country is considered a bad way to be. On the one hand, you're expected to hide it, feel ashamed of it, even deny it. I didn't feel ashamed of who I was, that was my punishment.'

'But you went to college?' he added.

'Yes I did,' she said, 'despite what happened.' Jessica continued, 'It says on my records that people believed I was not suitable for any sort of education because of my background.'

Another one of the men addressed her. 'We understand that this is very difficult for you. Your endeavours and what you have achieved are admirable.'

'Please don't patronise me,' she screamed, 'it only adds to my shame.' In her mind, she was thinking what am I doing here? All settled people in the room. Three men quizzing her about her Traveller identity, her abuse, her lack of education and so on. In her mind, the questions were getting louder. 'Keep them in,' she repeatedly counselled herself.

But she was unable to hold the voices in, so she reminded herself why she was here in this room. How could she trust these settled people to understand how she felt?

Then she blurted out, 'This is bigger than me. Traveller kids died because of this stuff. I'm bearing witness to my history and that of my peers in honouring Travellers who were mistreated in care, who are now dead. I'm alive. I need to deposit my guilt of survival.' Jessica relived her nightmare in this room while everyone else was absorbed in a frenzy of notetaking.

She told them everything. How this process was hard, but that they made it harder because they were choosing to ignore a crucial element of her story – her Traveller identity, obvious and simple. 'The state or its civil servants and the people who ran and worked in institutions say they didn't recognise Travellers as being any different to other Irish people. Yet how come our abuse was motivated by who we were as evidenced by our surnames?' Jessica remarked.

'How come most of us ended up in psychiatric care? How come a lot of us couldn't tell our families that we'd been beaten, marked and stained by settled people? Your Honour, please explain why their beatings made us stupid?' She stopped. 'I know times were different back then, but I will always believe it was racism that fuelled their adrenalin to keep beating us until they saw blood.' There was silence in the room. Jessica kept speaking.

For the rest of her life, she will never fully understand what happened that day. Often when Jessica goes over everything in her head, she wonders if they were confused. Did they fully understand what had happened to her? A half of an apology, that was more than a lot of other Travellers ever got. They saw what they wanted to see, heard what they wanted to hear. But she too got what she needed. The settlement would never be a waiver of her Traveller identity. Jessica Ward's ethnicity had to be written into her file.

(Contributor's note: This piece is dedicated to M, with pride and gratitude.)

ALL ARE EQUAL BEFORE THE LAW AND ARE ENTITLED WITHOUT ANY DISCRIMINATION TO EQUAL PROTECTION OF THE LAW. ALL ARE ENTITLED TO EQUAL PROTECTION AGAINST ANY DISCRIMINATION IN VIOLATION OF THIS DECLARATION AND AGAINST ANY INCITEMENT TO SUCH DISCRIMINATION.

ARTICLE 7

Liam Herrick

Executive Director of the Irish Penal Reform Trust

The language of human rights often evokes suspicions among traditionalists who see human rights standards as threatening to supplant older established moral values. In a rapidly changing world, such fears are understandable, but the history of how our human rights laws came about tells quite a different story. In fact, the bite-sized articles of the Universal Declaration of Human Rights draw their inspiration from the moral precepts of the main religious and philosophical traditions. And, just like the major religious texts they draw their inspiration from, the power of the articles lies in using simple language to express ambitious and complex ideas.

Nowhere is this more evident than in the ideas about law and justice contained in Article 7. Reading the carefully drafted words of the article, on one hand we have the idea of an impartial and even-handed Justice – the image of Justice personified as blind to the influence of those who stand before her. On the other hand, we see the idea of Justice as a protector of those vulnerable to victimisation – the image of Justice extending the protective shield of law over the weak. The imagery is simple, but this article continues to resonate because it is just as challenging for governments today as it was in 1948. It requires fair laws but also action to make law effective and, ultimately, it contains a political demand that all parts of society should be treated fairly.

At the level of formal law, the ideas in Article 7 provide a neat legend for the struggles against prejudice and intolerance that dominated global and national history for the second part of the twentieth century. Stark institutional forms of discrimination against women and against racial and ethnic minorities were confronted and overcome by the power of the rule of law. Apartheid was toppled, national laws excluding women from work or from public office were repealed and electoral systems that preferred one religious or political minority were reformed. In all parts of the globe, dramatic progress has been made in making the content of codified law fulfil the aspiration of equality.

Removing clear-cut legal discrimination, such as the South African race laws or Northern Ireland's electoral laws, were critical and necessary steps, but we see now how civil rights once legislated for must be nurtured. In many respects, law reform is the easiest aspect of what was demanded by the drafters of Article 7. The struggles to replace institutional prejudice in the written law have exposed the depth and complexity of the forms of discrimination and denials of human rights. The crucial feature of the equality guarantee is that it is about much more than formal or legalistic equality. It is about ensuring that those inequalities are deconstructed and removed in practice, and the more difficult challenge for a just society lies in making equality a reality rather than a paper exercise.

In Ireland, our Constitution of 1937 contains an explicit equality guarantee. A strong body of anti-discrimination law has been introduced since the 1970s, but legislation has still not succeeded, for example, in preventing all employers from dismissing pregnant workers or in preventing businesses from denying service to members of the Traveller community. Clearly, legislating for equality must be accompanied by measures creating the conditions whereby good law can be effective. The work of bodies such as the Equality Authority, the Mental Health Commission, the Ombudsman and the Irish Human Rights Commission combined with the work of agencies such as the Legal Aid Board is crucial in assisting marginalised groups and individuals to benefit from the progressive laws that have been introduced. Unfortunately, as we enter into a period of economic instability when the marginalised will be increasingly at risk, the current government has recently moved to undermine many of the bodies needed to make equality a reality rather than an aspiration.

More worrying still is the continuing vulnerability of groups hidden in the more obscure closed spaces of our society where the reach of the law's protection is still not felt. In our nursing homes, prisons and psychiatric hospitals, access to justice remains an aspiration and we are continuing to confront the awful violations of human dignity that have occurred and continue to occur in state-funded institutions. The scandals of our recent past have demonstrated most painfully how society as a whole has a duty to seek out and investigate violations of rights and to ensure that the vulnerable are protected. We cannot wait for the voiceless to access the law's protection themselves. The recent moves to establish investigative and oversight bodies for residential institutions and places of detention will, in time, bring the cold eye of the law into areas of Irish life that, in the past, society was happy to conceal, breathing life into the aspiration of equal protection contained in our laws. In this area, the work of the investigations into historical abuses in residential settings and the recent establishment of bodies such as the Garda Síochána Ombudsman Commission and Inspector of Prisons give us real cause for optimism.

For those in privileged positions in society, including those in government, perhaps the most onerous of the challenges contained in Article 7 is to agree to be bound by the same force of law that they apply to others. Tracing this guarantee back to its Christian origins, Article 7 asks that we 'do unto others as we would have done unto ourselves'. The statue of the blindfolded Justice that stands over the Four Courts in Dublin represents the superficially straightforward ideal that all of us are looked on equally by the law. In reality, the sections of society that wield law's power impose quite different standards and consequences on different groups in society.

Far from being blind, criminal law is applied inconsistently, seeking out certain groups for harsh punishment often in a most vivid way. The levels of contact that young people have with police and the attitude of the police towards them can vary dramatically across different communities. Social welfare fraud, non-payment of fines or the commission of minor offences against property regularly lead the poor and marginalised into the rudimentary chaos of our district courts, where the practice of law is swift and abrupt and the summary transfer onwards to the doors of our prisons is routine.

In contrast, the middle-class youth who gets into trouble with the law can expect a quite different experience. Minor misbehaviour is unlikely to attract police attention and, if it does, warnings will be exhausted before any actions are taken. In the exceptional case of such a youth coming before the courts, s/he can rely on character testimony from doctors and teachers and can avoid a criminal record by exploiting the court poor box system. Pleadings are made about the detrimental impact that a conviction will have on future travel opportunities, etc. and stern words from the bench are deemed sufficient punishment.

In terms of adult offenders, the theft of small amounts of property is treated as a serious crime, but when the transgression involves tax evasion or political corruption, the offender passes (at least initially) through the arches of Dublin Castle to a very different type of law. For this category of wealthy transgressor, barristers mill around wigged and gowned and gardaí are present only to keep the journalists at bay.

Despite some recent work of value in this area, there is a deficit in hard data on Irish sentencing practices, but practitioners strongly suspect that even in relation to 'ordinary crime' there are tangible differences in the penalties imposed on the guilty across the social classes. Studies profiling our prison population show that prisoners are almost universally drawn from a small number of acutely deprived urban centres, with intellectual disability, a family history of alcohol and drug abuse, and mental illness being the dominant characteristics of this group.

To paraphrase a famous Indian lawyer, the goal of equality before the law in society is such a wonderful and non-controversial idea, that it is a great shame that no one has succeeded in putting it into practice. Ireland has made much progress over the past sixty years in building the legal framework for equality and equal protection of law. The challenge now for government and society at large lies in how far we have to go in building the bridge from a society with many good laws to the fair society that expresses the real justice envisaged by Article 7.

EVERYONE HAS THE RIGHT TO AN EFFECTIVE REMEDY BY THE COMPETENT NATIONAL TRIBUNALS FOR ACTS VIOLATING THE FUNDAMENTAL RIGHTS GRANTED HIM BY THE CONSTITUTION OR BY LAW.

ARTICLE 8

Noeline Blackwell

Director General of FLAC (Free Legal Advice Centres Ltd)

Many would agree with Dickens's comment that the law is an ass, but would equally agree with Shakespeare that good counsellors lack no clients. Many people fear and distrust the law and lawyers. They will say that there is too much litigation but, if pushed, will equally recognise that any civilised state needs systems where those who are injured by injustice or abuse of power can make their complaint and receive a just remedy.

Given this common understanding, it might seem that Article 8 of the Universal Declaration of Human Rights is simply stating the obvious and is almost superfluous in the text of the declaration. What possible argument could there be with the sentiment that everyone has the right to an effective remedy before competent national tribunals for violations of a person's fundamental human rights?

The Irish legal system clearly does recognise the state's obligations under Article 8 of the UDHR. Ireland's written Constitution of 1937 provides for independent national courts. Court judgments have recognised and enforced the right to challenge the state for failure to vindicate fundamental rights, and have ordered remedial action where rights have been violated by those charged with protecting them. The constitutional structure requires judges to be independent of bureaucrats and politicians. More modern systems of redress, such as the Equality Tribunal and the Office of Ombudsman, aim to provide appropriate adjudication and remedies for such matters as unlawful discrimination and maladministration. Ireland, it would seem, is luckier and safer than many other countries.

Inevitably, Article 8 rights are not enjoyed equally by everyone in the state. The sixtieth anniversary of the UDHR is an opportunity to contrast the commitments Ireland has made with the reality of the uneven enjoyment of the rights contained in Article 8. It invites us to reflect on some further steps that are needed to bring that reality into a closer alignment with our commitments.

Justice is often compared to a five-star hotel where, at first glance, the doors seem to be open to everyone. It is only as you approach, or enter, that you realise that you can afford to do nothing without money and resources. When Cork woman Josie Airey complained to the European Court of Human Rights in the 1970s that she had no effective access to law in the context of a marital separation because she had no money for a solicitor, the Irish government's response was that she was perfectly entitled to represent herself before any court. Recognising that the right of access to a lawyer was a fundamental part of the right to a fair hearing and finding against Ireland, the European Court made a statement of principle that remains current today. It stated plainly that rights guaranteed (by the ECHR) were not to be rights 'that are theoretical or illusory but rights that are practical and effective'. Following that case, a civil legal aid scheme for those of modest means was established.

Today, the scheme provides important legal aid and advice to some low-income clients who are aware of its existence and can access its services despite its very restrictive financial eligibility test. But, significantly from the point of view of Article 8, even those who qualify under the means test may not get legal aid because certain areas of law are entirely excluded from the scheme. As a result, many face eviction from their homes or adjudication of their employment dismissal claims without access to legal advice or court representation. Some of these cases are straightforward, but some are not. But the current situation, where access to a lawyer is denied just because the problem falls into one area of law rather than another, denies many people that fundamental right to an effective remedy guaranteed by Article 8 of the UDHR.

The development of human rights in Ireland has depended to a great degree on the courts interpreting the law and Constitution dynamically in the light of generally progressive principles and changing times. However, the cost of engaging with the law or the legal system can act as a barrier to people, resulting in their not seeking a remedy at all.

In the Irish legal system, the person who loses a case is normally responsible for all of the costs. A judge may decide not to follow the normal rule on a discretionary basis where, despite the outcome, it is recognised that the case needed to be taken in the public interest to bring clarity to the extent of a fundamental right. But that decision will only be made at the end of a case once the risk, which can be enormous, has been assumed by the claimant. Limiting the costs associated with litigation through, for example, facilitating class action, is not an option in the Irish system and rules which might 'cap' costs are only in their infancy. Indeed, as if to emphasise this tendency, the newly introduced Immigration, Residence and Protection Bill not only restricts time limits and court procedures to vindicate immigrant rights, but also proposes unique additional penalties on lawyers acting for immigrants should they lose a case. It is inevitable that the intended dissuasive impact of this provision will result in the denial of rights to those with legitimate entitlements by impeding their access to any effective remedial mechanism.

But it's not all bad news. Following the incorporation of the European Convention on Human Rights into Irish law in 2003, Irish courts may now declare a law incompatible with the convention and the government, acting on the advice of the Attorney General, may decide to pay ex gratia compensation to the person who brought the action. Whether or not this remedy and other provisions of the ECHR Act 2003 bring real added human rights value remains to be seen.

Thus far, I have dealt with difficulties that might lie in the path of someone seeking an effective remedy before the competent national tribunals. The final issue which remains is the puzzle about how Article 8 interacts with rights that are sometimes characterised as purely 'political' claims beyond the remit of the courts. The distinction between those that the court can address, the so-called 'justiciable rights', and those other 'non-justiciable' rights or political claims is often unclear. A broad distinction can, however, be discerned between those rights that are categorised as 'civil and political' and thereby justiciable and those that are categorised as socio-economic and thereby non-justiciable. In other words, a claim founded on civil and political rights can be vindicated by a court, but one founded on socio-economic rights cannot. This is not a distinction that would be readily understood in most of the world's legal systems where rights are guaranteed on the understanding that, regardless of categorisation, human rights are indivisible. Nonetheless, this distinction affects many who seek an effective remedy for the violation of their rights, however categorised.

In one of the more trenchant assertions of this position, which remains a strongly embedded orthodoxy in this state, former Minister for Justice, Equality and Law Reform, Michael McDowell, wrote: 'I firmly believe that it is for the legislature to decide whether minimum guaranteed standards of social and economic justice should be established in law.' That is as may be. Article 8 does not provide an alternative view of the separation of powers, but it does demand that effective remedies are available through a competent national tribunal. The question, therefore, that arises for the legislature and the government is how to provide effective remedies through competent national tribunals for violations of fundamental socio-economic rights if these are never to be provided by the courts. Currently, there is no clear answer to this question, apart from the broad argument that the condition of the marginalised must be addressed primarily through politics. The fact that the condition of the marginalised may be hard evidence of a real political systems failure with no meaningful possibility of a justice check by the courts points to a substantial gap in human rights protection in Ireland.

When the UDHR was being debated, Eleanor Roosevelt, one of its guiding lights and the US representative, initially suggested that there was no specific need to include Article 8 in the text because the rights it contained were a prerequisite to the realisation of the other rights in the declaration. Following debate, she agreed that the article should be included, and it was passed unanimously and without abstention by the UN General Assembly. As circumstances have shown, this enabling right can be overlooked. When it is, those who tend to lose out are those without strong resources. Therefore, the challenge is to promote this right, not as one of arid principle, but as a right that is essential to the realisation of the other rights of the vulnerable and voiceless in society.

NO ONE SHALL BE SUBJECTED TO ARBITRARY ARREST, DETENTION OR EXILE.

ARTICLE 9

Dr Kathleen Cavanaugh

Irish Centre for Human Rights, NUI Galway, and Chairperson of Amnesty International Ireland

The 'war on terror' discourse suggests a conflict between human rights and the needs of state security. A politics of fear, which accompanies this discourse, has created a space where there has been a virtual rewriting of international law. The human rights community, far from celebrating sixty years of progress since the adoption of the Universal Declaration of Human Rights, finds itself in hostile political terrain. Against this backdrop, the very limits of international legal norms are being tested, perhaps nowhere more evident than when addressing the right to personal liberty.

Article 9 of the UDHR contains four essential concepts: (a) 'arbitrary'; (b) 'arrest'; (c) 'detention'; and (d) 'exile'. Each of these concepts, when evaluated, provides direction about how, when applied, this particular right is to be interpreted. The United Nations Committee on the Study of the Right of Everyone to Be Free from Arbitrary Arrest, Detention and Exile has indicated that there are two elements to the definition of 'arrest'. The first relates to the *manner* in which the arrest is affected and, secondly, the *length of time* for which a suspect can be held in custody. Similarly, the committee has defined detention as: 'The act of confining a person to a certain place, whether or not in continuation of arrest, and under restraints which prevent him from living with his family or carrying out his normal occupational or social activities.'

The drafters of the UDHR and, subsequently, the International Covenant on Civil and Political Rights (ICCPR) understood that it would not be possible or desirable to prohibit any form of detention or arrest, so they introduced the concept of 'arbitrariness'. This qualifier would, however, ignite debate about its meaning and the precise extent to which it qualified the arrest and detention prohibitions. Does the word 'arbitrary' mean simply 'unlawful' or does it impose a higher international standard which provides for both a substantive as well as procedural guarantee?

If arbitrary merely implies 'unlawful' or 'illegal', then the prohibition under Article 9 would be limited to government action that was unlawful and not to government action that may have been prescribed by law, but which is oppressive. If, however, the word 'arbitrary' suggests a higher international standard – above that which is provided for under domestic law – then this suggests that Article 9 envisages not only that a person is free from deprivation of liberty that is unlawful, but that such a detention must not be oppressive and must conform to international standards, which endeavour to optimise the right to personal liberty.

In reviewing the legislative drafting history of Article 9 of the UDHR, it is clear that the drafters intended a broader interpretation of what constitutes arbitrariness. They intended that the right to be free from arbitrary arrest and detention or exile must be understood *within the context* of securing the right to personal liberty. The drafters were not unaware – and, indeed, this was made clearer in the drafting of the ICCPR – that challenges to state authority and security may test the bounds of these rights. But, as with the drafting of Article 9(1) of the ICCPR that would follow, a person's security and liberty must be protected from the arbitrariness of state action and this would entail both a substantive as well as procedural obligation on the part of the state.

Article 9(1) of the ICCPR gives 'legal legs' to the rights expressed under Article 9 of the UDHR. It states that: 'Everyone has the right to liberty and security of person. No one shall be subjected to arbitrary arrest or detention. No one shall be deprived of his liberty except on such grounds and in accordance with such procedure as are established by law.' The UN Human Rights Committee (HRC) commentary on Article 9(1) indicates that this paragraph applies to 'all deprivations of liberty, whether in criminal cases or in other cases such as, for example, mental illness, vagrancy, drug addiction, educational purposes, immigration control, etc.'. The committee went on to note that 'the important guarantee laid down in paragraph 4, i.e. the right to control by a court of the legality of the detention, applies to all persons deprived of their liberty by arrest or detention'. This outlines the procedural guarantee noted earlier.

So, if we understand the right to be free from arbitrary detention, arrest and exile as including two sets of rights, both substantive and procedural, how has this right been promoted and protected in the Irish context? The domestic provisions which prohibit arbitrary detention are to be found under Article 40.4.1° of the Irish Constitution 1937, which states: 'No citizen shall be deprived of his personal liberty save in accordance with law.' However, if we review the current landscape in Ireland in 2009, there are areas where state practice fails to comply with international standards: in relation to prolonged periods of detention, in relation to the detention of the mentally ill and 'at risk' children, the use of Irish airports for rendition flights, and in relation to immigration-related detention

There are three pieces of legislation that have provisions which allow for prolonged periods of detention: section 30(4A) of the Offences Against the State Act 1939, as amended by the Offences Against the State (Amendment) Act 1998, section 50 of the Criminal Justice Act 2007 and the Criminal Justice (Drug Trafficking) Act 1996 (although this particular act is rarely used). The 1998 Act allowed for an increased period of detention without charge, while the 2007 Act extended the categories of offences for which a person could be held without charge, and extended the period of detention *without charge* for up to seven days. Under section 30(1) of the Offences Against the State Act 1939, a person may be arrested on suspicion of being about to commit an offence.

If we measure these provisions and practices against the requirements of UDHR Article 9 (read with 9(1) of the ICCPR), several difficulties arise. Firstly, the wording of the 2007 Act is particularly problematic as, under section 50, a person may be arrested and detained *solely* on the authority of a garda officer of the rank of chief superintendent or above. When in custody, a person may be held for up to forty-eight hours without being brought before a judge (under section 50(3)(g) and (h)) and for a period of up to seven days in total without charge. While international monitoring bodies do give state authorities a margin of appreciation for extending periods of detention without charge when they are facing a valid state of emergency, ten years after the signing of the Good Friday Agreement 1998, it is hard to argue that Ireland faces such a threat. With regard to the question of preventative detention, the UN HRC, which is the treaty monitoring body of the ICCPR, has previously expressed concern that this provision of Irish law is not compatible with Article 9.

The use of Irish airports as a transport point for rendition flights has been the subject of much debate both within Irish government and civil society. While diplomatic assurances from the US, which maintains that no flights transporting detainees have passed through Irish airports, have been accepted by the state, these assurances have failed to satisfy either the HRC

(2008 Concluding Comments) or the Special Rapporteur on Torture. There are both positive and negative obligations on the part of a state with regard to its international legal commitments. So, in this case, Ireland must not only ensure that the US declares rendition flights (which is, admittedly, reliant on the good faith declarations), but it must take proactive steps to ensure that its territory is not used for the purpose of rendition flights and to conduct investigations where allegations of such flights are made. It must also be borne in mind that many of those who have been subject to extraordinary rendition were arbitrarily arrested and detained, held without charge or due process and taken to countries where they faced torture.

The Mental Health Act 2001 allows for involuntary detention of mentally ill persons. Part II of the Act, which came into force in 2006, ostensibly provides better rights protection for those in-patients or those involuntarily detained, but it remains unclear if this has translated into a more transparent way of assessing the criteria (e.g. 'serious likelihood', 'immediate and serious harm' and 'serious deterioration in his or her condition') by which the Mental Heath Tribunal assesses the lawfulness of involuntary detention. The admission of children also raises concerns under Article 9. A child may be detained on the request of a parent or a person acting *in loco parentis*, without the child's own consent, even if the child is competent to make his or her own decisions. As noted by the HRC commentary, protection against an arbitrary deprivation of liberty is not only relevant in criminal cases, but applies equally to all forms of detention by a state, including detention for reasons of mental illness.

Ireland's policy of placing children considered to be 'at risk' in penal institutions as an 'interim custody' measure 'for the purpose of' an educational supervisory regime, despite the fact that their detention was not the result of being charged with or convicted of a crime, raises serious questions under Article 9. This practice continues despite a 2002 European Court of Human Rights ruling in *D.G. vs. Ireland*, in which the court argued that while a state could order a child to be detained to protect his/her welfare, they could not order that child to be detained in a penal institution when they have committed no crime. The court noted that international legal standards imposed a relationship between the grounds for permitted detention and the type of detention imposed. Additionally, the court noted that if the Irish state chose a constitutional system of educational supervision implemented through court orders to deal with juvenile delinquency, it was obliged to put in place appropriate institutional facilities which met the security and educational demands of that system in order to satisfy the requirements of Article 5 of the ECHR, which reflects the provisions of Article 9 of the UDHR and 9(1) of the ICCPR. The court determined that, in this case, St Patrick's Institution – which was the detention centre in question and continues to be a holding centre for minors in Ireland – was a penal institution and, as such, did not provide the necessary educational supervision.

Finally, the question of arbitrary arrest and detention arises within the Irish context with regard to immigration-related detention. The Irish Council for Civil Liberties has noted that immigration-related detention is on the rise. Its legal provisions are found under section 5(1) of the Immigration Act 1999, section 7 of the Immigration Act 2004 and sections 55 and 56 of the Immigration, Residence and Protection Bill 2008. Immigrants may be detained at the time of arrival, during processing (to determine status) and when awaiting removal from the state. Article 9 issues arise with regard to conditions of detention (because there arc no special detention facilities for immigrants and a majority are detained in penal institutions), length of detention and the right to be informed in a language understood so that s/he can challenge the lawfulness of detention.

The safeguard against arbitrary action by a state is fundamental to human rights law. Where tensions between domestic and international practices arise, as is often the case when it comes to situations of arrest and detention, a state must ensure that its practices are compliant with its international legal obligations. Within the Irish context, a review of Article 9 compliance suggests that in four primary areas – rendition flights, immigration-related detention, detention based on state security and detention for those deemed to be 'at risk' – the state has failed to adequately protect those under its jurisdiction.

EVERYONE IS ENTITLED IN FULL EQUALITY TO A FAIR AND PUBLIC HEARING BY AN INDEPENDENT AND IMPARTIAL TRIBUNAL, IN THE DETERMINATION OF HIS RIGHTS AND OBLIGATIONS AND OF ANY CRIMINAL CHARGE AGAINST HIM.

ARTICLE 10

Michael Farrell

Solicitor, FLAC and member of the Irish Human Rights Commission

'The Worst Miscarriage of Justice of All Time'

On 5 October 1975, Lesley Molseed, an eleven-year-old schoolgirl, disappeared on her way to do a message in Rochdale, near Manchester. Three days later, her body was found on nearby moorland. She had been stabbed twelve times and sexually assaulted.

The whole community was shocked and frightened by Lesley's brutal murder. The police were under pressure to find the killer quickly. Their suspicions focused on Stefan Kiszko, the twenty-four-year-old son of Ukrainian immigrants. He was a big, overweight and childish man. He had a learning disability and a mental age of twelve. He lived at home with his mother. He was a bit 'different'.

Three teenage girls told police that Stefan Kiszko had exposed himself to them and had stalked one of them. The police found he had written down the number of a car that had been sighted near the murder scene.

Mr Kiszko was arrested on 21 December 1975. He was upset and confused and asked to see his mother. The police refused. They did not tell him he was entitled to see a solicitor and, after two days of questioning, he admitted to Lesley's murder. He later protested his innocence and said the police had told him that, if he confessed, he would be allowed to go home for Christmas.

He was charged and remanded in custody. In July 1976, he was convicted and sentenced to life imprisonment. When he returned to prison, he was badly beaten by other prisoners for being a child killer. After that, he lived in fear and spent most of his time in prison in solitary confinement for his own safety. After three or four years, he developed schizophrenia and suffered from delusions. Eventually, he was placed in a secure mental hospital.

Stefan Kiszko's mother worked tirelessly to prove her son's innocence. She got a new solicitor, Campbell Malone, to take up the case and, in 1991, he persuaded the British Home Office to reopen it. It quickly emerged that the police had had evidence all along that showed that Mr Kiszko could not have been the killer.

Traces of semen had been found on Lesley Molseed's under-clothes. The semen contained sperm, but Stefan Kiszko suffered from a condition that made him infertile. He could not produce sperm. The semen could not have come from him. This evidence had never been shown to the defence or to the court.

The prosecution case quickly fell apart. The three girls who had claimed Mr Kiszko had exposed himself to them admitted that they had made up the story. Mr Kiszko had an innocent explanation for having the number of the suspicious car. His conviction was quashed in February 1992, after sixteen years in jail. It was another few months before he was well enough to be released from hospital.

He went back to his mother's house, but he was confused and frightened and rarely went out. His health never recovered, and he died of a heart attack a little over a year after he was released. He was forty-one. His mother, worn out, died four months later at the age of seventy.

Stefan Kiszko had been due to receive £500,000 in compensation for his wrongful imprisonment but he and his mother died before they could claim it. An outspoken Conservative MP, with under-standable emotion, described the case as 'the worst miscarriage of justice of all time'.

In November 2007, fifteen years after Stefan Kiszko was released, Ronald Castree, a convicted sex offender who had lived in the same estate as Lesley Molseed, was convicted of her murder. He had been arrested after an unrelated incident, but his DNA was found to be an exact match to the traces left by Lesley's killer. It was a salutary reminder that wrongful convictions not only affect the person convicted, but may mean that the real perpetrator walks free.

'Perjured into Prison'

Around the same time as Stefan Kiszko was released in 1992, another miscarriage of justice was in the making in Donegal. Gardaí had begun a series of raids on The Point Inn, a pub and nightclub at Quigley's Point, close to Derry, looking for drugs. Eventually, they charged the publican, Frank Shortt, with knowingly allowing the sale of drugs on his premises.

The case was due for hearing in October 1994, but prosecuting counsel pointed out that there was no evidence in the garda statements to show that Mr Shortt was aware that drugs were being sold. The gardaí involved went away and, in the words of Mr Justice Hardiman in a Supreme Court judgment in March 2007, 'engaged in a conspiracy to transform a very weak case into a very strong one by inventing evidence'.

When the case went to trial in February 1995, Mr Shortt protested his innocence, but the new evidence was given, and he was convicted and sentenced to three years' imprisonment. He was 'perjured into prison', as Judge Hardiman put it in a swingeing critique in the Supreme Court. The conviction was upheld on appeal.

Frank Shortt was sixty when he went to jail. He was married with five children, two of them still teenagers. He found prison very hard, especially at the start when held in filthy conditions in Mountjoy. He suffered badly from depression and stress and, later, from a heart condition.

His business collapsed and his pub was burned down, seemingly by the IRA, because of his conviction for drug-dealing. His children were taunted and bullied at school, and his family relationships deteriorated.

Frank Shortt served his full sentence and, when he came out, he was in poor health; he could not get a job; and had to live on disability benefit. He was withdrawn and depressed but deter-mined to prove his innocence, and the case went back to the Court of Criminal Appeal in November 2000.

By then the whole saga of corruption within the gardaí in Donegal had begun to unfold and the DPP consented to the quashing of Frank Shortt's conviction, but with no explanation of what had happened.

Two years later, in 2002, after a long and strenuously contested hearing, the Court of Criminal Appeal certified that Mr Shortt had been the victim of a miscarriage of justice. The court had heard how a garda superintendent and a detective sergeant had fabricated statements, concealed evidence and lied to the court to secure his conviction. Judge Hardiman noted wryly that the culprits 'bore him no personal ill-will [but acted] in pursuit of an unscrupulous scheme to advance their careers'.

It was another five years before the Supreme Court, in March 2007, finally awarded Frank Shortt €4,623,871 in compensation and damages for what the Chief Justice described as 'a pot of iniquity' by the gardaí concerned. It was fifteen years since the gardaí had started their series of raids on The Point Inn.

For most people, miscarriages of justice probably mean high-profile 'political' cases like the Birmingham Six or Guildford Four in Britain, or the Sallins mail train case here in Ireland. But the Kiszko and Shortt cases show that miscarriages of justice can happen to anybody: a shy, vulnerable man with a learning disability like Stefan Kiszko, or someone like Frank Shortt who just happened to be a convenient target for a couple of ambitious and unscrupulous police officers out to boost their careers.

That is why we need, and need to defend, 'the right to a fair and public hearing by an independent and impartial tribunal' as required by Article 10 of the Universal Declaration of Human Rights, with all the seemingly technical and tiresome rules of evidence and fair procedures that go with such tribunals and courts.

And because courts can make mistakes as well – and did in the Kiszko and Shortt cases – we need fall-back systems to reopen and re-examine alleged miscarriages of justice, as happened in those cases. Lord Denning famously said it would be 'an appalling vista' if the Birmingham Six were found to have been wrongly convicted. It would be a more appalling vista if innocent people could be railroaded into prison without redress, through ignorance, prejudice or just because they are available, while the actual perpetrators are not pursued.

(1) EVERYONE CHARGED WITH A PENAL OFFENCE HAS THE RIGHT TO BE PRESUMED INNOCENT UNTIL PROVED GUILTY ACCORDING TO LAW IN A PUBLIC TRIAL AT WHICH HE HAS HAD ALL THE GUARANTEES NECESSARY FOR HIS DEFENCE.

(2) NO ONE SHALL BE HELD GUILTY OF ANY PENAL OFFENCE ON ACCOUNT OF ANY ACT OR OMISSION WHICH DID NOT CONSTITUTE A PENAL OFFENCE, UNDER NATIONAL OR INTERNATIONAL LAW, AT THE TIME WHEN IT WAS COMMITTED. NOR SHALL A HEAVIER PENALTY BE IMPOSED THAN THE ONE THAT WAS APPLICABLE AT THE TIME THE PENAL OFFENCE WAS COMMITTED.

ARTICLE 11

Fr Peter McVerry SJ

Founder of the Peter McVerry Trust

The 'presumption of innocence' has been a cornerstone of Irish law for centuries. 'Innocent until proven guilty' is a phrase that even children are familiar with. Within the legal process, this principle imposes a very clear responsibility on the prosecution authorities to prove a person's guilt beyond all reasonable doubt. Since no legal system is perfect and injustices may inevitably occur from time to time, the law seeks to ensure that no innocent person will be convicted, even if that concern sometimes results in the guilty going free.

However, the presumption of innocence is under strain in Ireland, as elsewhere. As the level of violence in our society increases, people feel more and more insecure and are not very supportive of what they perceive to be abstract principles that may increase risks to them. As people grow wealthier, they have more to protect. Others, particularly those who are 'different', who belong to a different social class or who are labelled in one way or another, are seen as a threat to be kept at arm's length – or preferably even farther away – by any means necessary. Others may consider the threat of terrorism to be so serious that the sacrifice of the liberty of a few innocents can appear as a small price to pay for the security of many.

The media – in tabloid and other formats – have contributed in no small way to the erosion of respect for the presumption of innocence. In a number of high-profile criminal cases where the accused was acquitted, some newspapers have continued to write about the accused in such a way as to characterise the verdict as a travesty of justice. In other gang-related incidents, individuals have been profiled as 'gang leaders', often glamorised by the use of nicknames, leaving readers in no doubt as to their involvement in serious crime. Any previous conviction by a suspected gang member is sufficient to label them as a likely future crime player and threat to society. 'Trial by media' has become a normal part of life for some. This kind of reporting of crime feeds into the growing sense of insecurity that people feel and thereby ensures good and steady sales for media products engaged in sensationalised crime reporting.

The desire to give more rights to victims of crime is something that everyone wants to support. However, it can often be presented as if in opposition to the rights of the accused. The public perception may be that the law is too heavily weighted towards the interests of the latter and that the rights of victims are not sufficiently recognised or protected. This perception is heightened when a high-profile criminal case is dismissed on 'technicalities'. In such cases, many feel that justice for the victim has been denied by the absurd application of the letter of the law, and that the law, whose function is to ensure that justice is applied to all in society, is, in fact, contributing to a serious injustice in this particular case or, indeed, systemically. This perception is shared and reflected by many in the media.

One such case was dismissed on the ground that the search warrant that was used to obtain evidence that was vital to the prosecution case was several hours out of date. However, these so-called 'technicalities' are a protection for all – the innocent as well as the guilty – to prevent abuse of the legal system and possible miscarriages of justice. Such cases, where the guilt or innocence of the accused is not determined by the presentation of the evidence in court because of some prior legal infringement of the rights of the accused, usually reveal an incompetence or inefficiency on the part of the investigation and/or prosecution authorities. The fact that evidence is illegally or unconstitutionally obtained is and ought to be of consequence. The public response, more appropriately, ought be to demand that the authorities carry out their responsibilities properly instead of seeking to undermine the protections which the law enshrines precisely for the purpose of preventing miscarriages of justice by the abuse of the law. Such protections ultimately guarantee the 'rule of law'.

It is, of course, entirely appropriate to seek to enhance the rights of victims. Where victims feel that their rights, or their voices, have not been given adequate attention by the justice system, then these feelings have to be considered. It may well be that the law should be changed, for example to give legal representation to the victims of serious crime. But the rights of the victims are not in opposition to the rights of the accused – it is not a question of 'balancing' those rights. It is rather a question of strengthening the rights of both victims and accused. The dissatisfaction that is sometimes expressed by victims and others is an important wake-up call to law makers and elected representatives to re-examine their obligation to ensure that the rights of the victims, and their need to be heard in the criminal process, are adequately protected. But it should not be a call to 'make it easier' to bring in guilty verdicts by diminishing the rights of the accused.

There has been much publicity recently in Ireland about politicians who have made representations to the courts or to the Minister for

Justice, Equality and Law Reform on behalf of those found guilty of a crime, sometimes a serious crime. Politicians have given letters of reference to be considered by the courts when imposing an appropriate punishment or have intervened to secure some advantage for those who have been imprisoned, such as early release from prison or transfer to a more liberal prison regime. People have expressed outrage at any such intervention. They have sometimes been motivated by the very admirable desire not to cause further pain to the victim by the perception that an important person in society is 'taking the side' of the offender. However, this outrage is often misplaced. No person, even those found guilty of serious crime, is all bad. There are positive aspects to their character or of their past behaviour that are entirely appropriate, indeed necessary for the effective administration of justice, to be placed before a judge prior to deciding on a sentence. While in prison, it is entirely appropriate that interventions from people who know the prisoner, seeking further rehabilitation opportunities within the prison system for the prisoner or seeking compassionate release to attend a funeral or visit a sick relative, should be made. The outrage may be justified, however, when the intervention is being made by a politician who does not personally know the prisoner but is writing a letter purely in their role as public representative at the request of some third party. But such outrage can lead to a demand for more repressive prison conditions for those convicted of serious crime and less concern for the rights and rehabilitation of the offender, neither of which is in the interests of society. Such a demand feeds into a desire for vengeance rather than a desire for justice.

The law is the only protection that people have against the abuse or misuse of power and the infringement of their rights. While it is essential that people have confidence in the law to protect them, and therefore that those who make and administer the law listen carefully to the concerns of ordinary citizens, the pressure to circumvent the law by 'cutting corners', or to bypass the law altogether through 'trial by media', will lead society down a dangerous path to a place where injustice may appear to be justice or where people take the law into their own hands.

NO ONE SHALL BE SUBJECTED TO ARBITRARY INTERFERENCE WITH HIS PRIVACY, FAMILY, HOME OR CORRESPONDENCE, NOR TO ATTACKS UPON HIS HONOUR AND REPUTATION. EVERYONE HAS THE RIGHT TO THE PROTECTION OF THE LAW AGAINST SUCH INTERFERENCE OR ATTACKS.

ARTICLE 12

John Saunders

Director of SHINE (formerly Schizophrenia Ireland)

Privacy in Mental Healthcare: A Privilege or a Right?

I wish to address two fundamental issues in Irish mental health care as they relate to the right to privacy enshrined in Article 12 of the Universal Declaration of Human Rights. The first is the scope of doctor–patient confidentiality in the context of mental health and the second is identifying a number of areas in which privacy rights are compromised in current mental health provision.

A number of international instruments address the right to privacy. Article 12 of the UDHR states that: 'No one shall be subjected to arbitrary interference with his privacy, family, home or correspondence, nor to attacks upon his honour and reputation. Everyone has the right to the protection of the law against such interference or attacks.' Article 17 of the International Covenant on Civil and Political Rights (ICCPR) provides in general terms that no one shall be subjected to arbitrary or unlawful interference with his privacy. Principle 13 of the UN Principles for the Protection of Persons with Mental Illness and the Improvement of Mental Health Care provides that every patient in a mental-health facility shall, in particular, have the right to full respect of his or her privacy. Other international conventions, such as the European Convention on Human Rights and, more recently, the UN Convention on the Rights of People with Disabilities, also reinforce this right explicitly.

For citizens of Western developed states such as Ireland, the right to privacy is often taken for granted. For the most part, a citizen's right to privacy is respected and upheld in law. Of course, there are always exceptions to the rule. One must be mindful of the fact that no right is absolute and issues consistently arise where society, and indeed the courts, must determine how to balance individual rights with public needs and balance competing rights of individuals. That said, particular attention is required to ensure that the rights of vulnerable groups, such as people who have a serious mental illness and who may use mental healthcare services from time to time, are adequately protected.

In the context of health, the right to privacy is central to the doctor–patient relationship, which ensures that any communication or interaction between the patient and his/her physician is bound by confidentiality and cannot be divulged to a third party without the express permission of the patient. Exceptions are recognised in particular cases of emergency. Nowhere is this rule of confidentiality more evident than in the area of mental health in the relationship between a mental healthcare patient and his or her consultant psychiatrist.

For most people, this relationship is uncontroversial. Difficulties can arise when a patient expressly wishes not to have information shared with his or her primary carer or family member. In the world of mental healthcare, people with the most dependent needs are often cared for, sometimes physically, by a family member, a spouse or a caring friend. In order for such carers to provide effective care and support, they may need to have access to some information about the well-being or otherwise of the individual. Problems arise when that information is not shared either because of express refusal by the patient to grant permission or because, in some cases, the physician may be of the view that sharing any information breaches the doctor–patient relationship. This latter situation may arise even where the patient has given permission for information to be disclosed.

There is an immediate and obvious dilemma for everyone involved here. On the one hand, there is an imperative to respect confidentiality, yet it must be acknowledged that a minimum level of information is often necessary to enable a carer to provide a reasonable and competent level of care. The common-sense approach is to ensure that only information that is essential to good care is shared. For example, practical matters, such as information about the condition, treatments, etc., are not necessarily confidential but may be significant for the carer. In some cases, however, the diagnosis or condition may be the very issue that the patient is disputing and does not want disclosed. At present, in the absence of consent of the patient, such information cannot and should not be disclosed without his or her consent.

One approach to resolving the dilemma is for the creation of agreed written protocols between the patient, his/her doctor and their family carer. This agreement can set out the amount of information to be shared and the circumstances in which it can be shared. Similarly, advanced directives can also be used to predetermine what happens if a person becomes mentally unwell in the future. An advanced directive is a statement of preference, specifying how a patient would want their treatment to be provided in the event of them losing the mental capacity to make such informed decisions. Advance directives may allow for proxies to be appointed and can also provide realistic safeguards to simple problems that might arise for the person with mental illness. Advanced directives are used in psychiatry in many countries and are legally binding. Unfortunately, the use of advanced directives in Ireland must await the introduction of legislation dealing with the issue of capacity to give a statutory basis for their implementation.

There is also a role for the regulators of medicine in Ireland, such as the Medical Council, in addressing this issue. It is my belief that scope exists for the creation of agreed protocols that allow doctors, under certain circumstances, to share information with close relatives or carers. Confidentiality in mental healthcare would be greatly facilitated by legislation underpinning the common law, international law and related ethical issues. Legislation could set out the conditions for legitimate disclosure of information.

Most models of mental healthcare now realise that the optimum level of good-quality care should be given in the community, where people can live as members of families and of their communities. In this scenario, it is essential that carers have access to appropriate information to enable them to discharge their caring role. This is a matter that needs clarification regarding the rights of the individual to privacy and the medical ethics relevant to doctor–patient confidentiality.

A separate but equally important issue is the protection of privacy rights of persons using the mental-health services. Any person using the mental-health services should be treated in the least restrictive environment, so that privacy, family rights and individual dignity are respected and maintained to the greatest extent possible.

A recent report on the concerns of service users and their carers published by the Mental Health Commission found that many service users reported that mental healthcare settings, both residential and day, don't offer a sufficient level of privacy. Often, for example, residents are not allowed to have personal or private space or their own personal possessions. Similarly, a report by the

Health Research Board on the quality of accommodation for people using community residences suggested that privacy was compromised and that people did not have an adequate level of privacy in what was essentially their own home. This is a direct contravention of Article 12 of the UDHR, which protects against arbitrary interference in the home.

The reasons for such a lack of privacy are primarily staff needs and the provision of institutional-type services to people in group homes. Issues of privacy were also highlighted in a survey undertaken in 2005 by the Mental Health Commission seeking service users' views on what constitutes quality in mental health-care services. Part of the requirement of a quality service is to provide settings and surroundings that respect the dignity of the individual, ensure basic comforts, meet needs and guarantee an acceptable level of privacy. This aspiration was translated into a fundamental principle in the *Mental Health Commission's Quality Framework for Mental Health Services* published following the consultation.

The physical conditions of older mental-health hospitals have been criticised for many years by the reports of the Inspector of Mental Hospitals and, more recently, by the Inspectorate of Mental Health Services. Conditions have been described as dehumanising and certainly do not live up to the standard required of a modern mental-healthcare service. Government must provide funding for the basic needs of patients to protect them from the effects of poor staffing, the lack of privacy and the diminution of their personal dignity. It is clear that if Ireland is to respect the spirit and letter of Article 12 of the UDHR, then every effort must be made by the state and its services to ensure that the right to privacy is maintained and actively protected at all times.

In any quality mental-health service, priority must be given to the protection of human rights, including the right to privacy, and this protection must be a priority in any discussion of resource allocation. Current financial difficulties should not be allowed to undermine people's human rights. The right to privacy is a fundamental right. In the area of mental health, where people are vulnerable for extended periods of time, it is essential that policy and practice protect privacy.

(1) EVERYONE HAS THE RIGHT TO FREEDOM OF MOVEMENT AND RESIDENCE WITHIN THE BORDERS OF EACH STATE.

(2) EVERYONE HAS THE RIGHT TO LEAVE ANY COUNTRY, INCLUDING HIS OWN, AND TO RETURN TO HIS COUNTRY.

ARTICLE 13

Salome Mbugua

National Director of AkiDwA

Freedom of movement is a right that every human being should be able to enjoy. Unfortunately, increased global migration and world events have resulted in the tightening of national borders.

A different approach to migration existed in 1994, when I first arrived as a student in Ireland from Kenya. At the time, I did not require a visa and only had to register myself with the Aliens Office, as it was called at the time, on Harcourt Street. In 1995, I left Ireland and, when I planned to visit the following year, I was told that I would need a visa. Countries had started to impose greater restrictions and it was becoming increasingly difficult for a person to enter Europe from other non-EEA countries, especially Africa. Approval for a visa was discretionary and could be refused with no explanation. I was grateful to be approved, but thereafter, it was necessary to obtain a visa whenever I entered or exited Ireland.

I acquired Irish citizenship in 2001. In 2004, I applied for a visa for my parents to visit my family and children in Ireland for a short period of two weeks. Even though I supplied the necessary documentation and the fact that my husband and daughters are Irish, and that I was an engaged and committed community-sector worker, my parents' visa to visit us was denied. After much delay and uncertainty, my local TD helped me to secure their visas through the proper channels. It is clear that, without intervention, I would not have been able to access a basic human right all of us treasure and aim to protect, that of freedom of movement.

Restrictive immigration policies of many European countries mean that more vulnerable people are not making it to safety and are being stopped at the border or detained before entry into a country. Some migrants detained are labelled 'illegal migrants', which, in the case of migrant women fleeing gender-based violence, might be because the system in their country of origin is not providing enough protection from the serious harm and persecution that might be unique to women's situations. International refugee law was initially developed largely on an understanding of the male migrant experience.

In detention centres, women often lack interpretation services and girls' education in their country of origin might have been negligible. There may also be no social workers available to handle cases of post-traumatic stress and the physical effects of gender-based violence. The depression and hopelessness created by insecure, inconsistent and non-transparent immigration processes, with protracted delays, can sometimes result in hunger strikes, self-harm and, in extreme cases, self-immolation.

Sadly, many women are treated with suspicion, distrust and dis-respect by officials dealing with their claims, which could be alleviated by the introduction of consistent, mandatory and monitored gender guidelines for asylum processes and procedures, which AkiDwA would like to see included in current immigration legislation.

AkiDwA currently works with women who entered their asylum claims in Ireland over five years ago and whose applications are still pending. These women's freedom of movement and choice has effectively been taken away and the majority survive on hope and faith. They hold on to the belief and the conviction that they will some day be able to rebuild their families' lives on the strong foundation of freedom and equal opportunity that exists in Ireland. But after so many years of waiting without further word, their resolve sometimes lessens and they can become quite discouraged.

Article 13 of the UDHR is meant to apply to each and every individual living in any given country that has signed up to the declaration, but Ireland chooses to apply it in what appears to be a discretionary manner. While it is not disputed that a country must have control of its immigration systems in order to effectively manage immigration, it must be stressed that the obligations of the UDHR cannot be displaced by this imperative.

Ireland is a country with a population of 4.2 million people, only a very small percentage of whom are asylum-seekers, and they do not represent a sizable proportion of immigrants living in Ireland. The expansion of EU borders has brought the biggest increase of immigrants, made up of new EU nationals, into Ireland. Ironically, there are fewer language problems with African migrants, as many African countries have English as their official language and Africans usually speak several other languages as well.

EU migrants and immigrants with residency status have the right to live anywhere within the twenty-six counties of Ireland, can access services, work or operate businesses and purchase property. In short, they are allowed to maintain themselves and their families. Asylum-seekers are restricted from free movement over great lengths of time. They are not permitted to be away from their accommodation, without express permission, for longer than three days, they are not allowed to work and are not allowed to move from the regional centre they have been assigned to except in exceptional circumstances.

Some people have been housed in regional accommodation centres for five years or more with only minimal welfare provisions.

Recent shifts in policy appear to be taking an even more restrictive stance against these long-term residents. Thus, the individuals who are most affected by a restriction of movement are those that the UDHR seeks most to protect: vulnerable people seeking protection from serious harm and persecution.

Since April 2000, the Irish government has operated a policy of dispersal and direct provision for asylum-seekers. After a short stay in a Dublin reception centre, asylum-seekers are dispersed to regional accommodation centres, some very remote and isolated and where a full range of community supports and services may not be available. Asylum-seekers are given full board (i.e. accommodation and meals) and an allowance of €19.10 per week (€9.60 per child). Successive ministers for Justice, Equality and Law Reform from 1999 onwards have characterised asylum-seekers as bogus, illegal migrants who exploit Ireland's welfare system. The welfare provided to asylum-seekers is well below what indigenous welfare recipients receive in emergency accommodation; it is a punitive welfare policy engaged by the state to discourage asylum-seekers.

Asylum-seekers who have fled their home countries to escape political or cultural persecution find themselves locked in limbo. Others have been deported back to countries of origin where some face the gender-based violence that precipitated their flight to safety in the first place. Individuals fleeing their countries in fear of their lives should not be criminalised nor suffer indignity or disrespect. Instead, they should be dealt with in a humane and fair manner reflecting the strong commitment to freedom that Irish history requires.

In an atmosphere where security controls are overriding basic protections, human rights activists in Europe are advocating for realistic and fair immigration policies where the right to freedom of movement in order to seek refuge from harm and persecution is respected. Many people will face persecution, torture or death if returned to their country of origin. Arrests on arrival are not uncommon and some of those returned may risk serious injury, long-term imprisonment or may even lose their lives. On 22 July 2008, forty-one people were deported from Ireland to Lagos, Nigeria, the result of a joint operation of nine European countries that included Ireland, France, Spain and Germany (*The Irish Times*, 24 July 2008). One such deportee, Rafiq Sjirinov, deported from Sweden during the mass deportation, was reportedly tortured and beaten to death upon his arrival in Azerbaijan.

Applying greater security controls while ignoring the very real situations of human beings in great need will not solve the migration problems that countries now face. In our divided globe, human rights are undermined when immigration polices do not reflect equality and fair access to justice. This is hardly what was intended by the drafters of Article 13 of the UDHR.

(1) EVERYONE HAS THE RIGHT TO SEEK AND TO ENJOY IN OTHER COUNTRIES ASYLUM FROM PERSECUTION.

(2) THIS RIGHT MAY NOT BE INVOKED IN THE CASE OF PROSECUTIONS GENUINELY ARISING FROM NON-POLITICAL CRIMES OR FROM ACTS CONTRARY TO THE PURPOSES AND PRINCIPLES OF THE UNITED NATIONS.

ARTICLE 14

Dr Maurice Manning

President of the Irish Human Rights Commission

The simple statement in Article 14(1) of the Universal Declaration of Human Rights (UDHR) that 'everyone has the right to seek and to enjoy in other countries asylum from persecution' is one that, today, most of us take for granted as a fundamental protection provided by the international community. Set down in the aftermath of the Second World War, Article 14 was an important and timely provision of the UDHR. Not only had the war created millions of refugees and displaced persons across Europe and Asia, but there had also been a catastrophic failure by the international community to protect whole populations from widespread and horrific persecution. Thus, Article 14 represented one of the most significant promises of the international community – that those fleeing persecution would be protected by the international community when they were not protected by their own state.

The promise of Article 14 was developed by the international community into what is still the cornerstone of refugee protection today, the 1951 Geneva Convention Relating to the Status of Refugees (Refugee Convention). It is interesting to recall that, when it was established, the 1951 Convention only concerned persons who became refugees in Europe because of events prior to 1 January 1951. Yet in the intervening sixty years since the adoption of the UDHR as a result of wars and unrest throughout the world, the refugee protection system developed into a permanent feature of the international human rights framework, with states putting complex systems in place to regulate asylum and refugee protection processes.

The commitment to safeguard individuals who are in danger and who are not protected by their own state is one which naturally flows from the pledge of the UDHR that all human beings have the right to life, liberty and security of person, and the right to live that life free from slavery, torture or cruel, inhuman or degrading treatment or punishment. However, in our modern world, the application of Article 14 is significantly more complicated than its simple opening provision would suggest.

Increasing globalisation and movement of people means that there is often a competing interest between regulation of economic migration and protection of refugees and asylum-seekers. We see that efforts to prevent and manage economic migration often conflict with effective refugee and asylum protection. While it must be acknowledged that systems need to be in place to regulate migration, such systems must not lessen our promise to those who seek protection. The terms 'refugee' and 'asylum-seeker' are weighed down with preconceptions and misconceptions. On the sixtieth anniversary of the UDHR, it is important to recall what we mean when we speak of refugees. We are referring to people who have a well-founded fear of persecution on the grounds of race, religion, nationality, membership of a particular social group or political opinion. We are referring to some of the world's most vulnerable people.

In Ireland, 2008 saw the proposal of new measures to regulate immigration, in the form of the Immigration, Residence and Protection Bill 2008. In providing observations on the provisions of the bill relating to refugees and asylum-seekers, the Irish Human Rights Commission (IHRC) expressed concern that the fundamental principle of refugee protection must not be diminished by any changes to the law. In particular, the IHRC was concerned that the bill would not in any way reduce the state's commitment to the principle of *non-refoulement* set out in Article 33 of the 1951 Refugee Convention. Article 33 prohibits the expulsion or return of a refugee in any manner whatsoever to the frontiers of territories where his life or freedom would be threatened on account of his race, religion, nationality, membership of a particular social group or political opinion. Article 33 may be said to provide substance to the protection principle set out in Article 14 of the UDHR.

Yet refugee protection in Ireland is subject to more than just these principles. I will not venture to cover all of them here, but I would recall that under the provisions of the European Convention on Human Rights and the International Covenant on Civil and Political Rights, everyone present in the state, whether present lawfully or unlawfully, is entitled to the protection of their human rights (as set out in those instruments), including the right not to be subjected to torture and other ill-treatment. As we stated in our observations, in the development of a consolidated immigration system in Ireland, there must not be any removal of the safeguards that currently exist, in particular the safeguards necessary to ensure that no one is subject to *refoulement*.

Human rights provisions in international treaties often represent the best intentions of the international community and the states that sign them. However, their protections require monitoring at the national level to ensure that states respect, by their national law, the promises they have made. The UDHR opens with the declaration:

> that every individual and every organ of society,
> [...] shall strive by teaching and education to
> promote respect for these rights and freedoms and
> by progressive measures, national and inter-

national, to secure their universal and effective recognition and observance, both among the peoples of Member States themselves and among the peoples of territories under their jurisdiction.

One of the most important 'progressive measures' of the last fifteen years has been the emergence of national human rights institutions (NHRI). NHRIs, such as the IHRC, are part of the fulfilment of the promise of the UDHR to promote respect for the rights and freedoms contained therein. When it adopted the Paris Principles in 1993, the UN General Assembly underlined its conviction that institutions at the national level can play a key role in promoting and protecting human rights and fundamental freedoms and in developing and enhancing public awareness of those rights and freedoms. NHRIs represent a concrete connection between a state's signature of an international treaty and the application of its provisions. Their existence and growth represent recognition that human rights require vigilance and independent oversight to secure their full realisation.

Today, there are over sixty national human rights institutions globally, including the Irish Human Rights Commission, which are fully in compliance with the roles and functions for NHRIs set out by the Paris Principles. These sixty institutions represent the growing trend towards the establishment and strengthening of national institutions. I believe that IHRC has a vital role in Ireland's human rights framework, in promoting respect for human rights and providing, as it does, independent and impartial advice to government on a wide range of human rights issues.

Central to our work are the principles set down sixty years ago in the UDHR.

It may, perhaps, seem a somewhat sad necessity that, in a document setting out the aspirations of humanity outlining how we should behave towards one another and whose first principle is that all humans are created equal in dignity and rights, it is also readily acknowledged that there will be instances where its provisions will not be respected and where action must be taken to protect those who suffer the violation of their rights. Yet, this is the case. Included with the positive rights elucidated in the UDHR is a right to seek protection from their violation. Some sixty years after its proclamation, there are millions of people around the world who do not enjoy the rights set out in the UDHR, and who need us to keep our promise.

Article 14(1) is a profoundly humanitarian provision. At its core is the understanding in Article 1 of the UDHR that all human beings are born free and equal in dignity and rights. Indeed, the promise of protection in Article 14 of the UDHR protects all of us. It represents the acceptance of a shared common responsibility all human rights are based on. It is also a recognition that the principles of the UDHR must be treated as positive obligations which require action on all our parts. On its sixtieth anniversary, the UDHR remains a source of guidance and inspiration for all of us, the template for a 'common standard of achievement for all peoples and all nations'. The Irish Human Rights Commission, working on its own and with others, strives to make this aspiration a reality for everyone in Ireland.

(1) EVERYONE HAS THE RIGHT TO A NATIONALITY.

(2) NO ONE SHALL BE ARBITRARILY DEPRIVED OF HIS NATIONALITY NOR DENIED THE RIGHT TO CHANGE HIS NATIONALITY.

ARTICLE 15

Dr Diarmuid Martin

Catholic Archbishop of Dublin

For most of us who live in Western democratic states, nationality is something we rarely think about except when we need a passport to go on holiday or, less happily, when something happens to us while we are on holiday. Otherwise, nationality rarely affects the way most of us live our day-to-day lives in any critical way.

Most of us are proud of our nationality. Hearing our national anthem played at an Olympic Games medal ceremony stirs up something within us that is linked with our cultural and historical identity. Competition in international sport is firmly anchored in the framework of nationality. Otherwise sober Irish citizens travel abroad donned in extraordinarily exuberant combinations of green on the occasion of international sporting events.

Nationality is, for most of our existence, experienced more as a cultural and emotive dimension of our lives than as a juridical or legal one. But when it comes to emotion, emotion about nationality can boil strongly. People go to war to defend their nationality and their right to preserve it. Genocide is often preceded and accompanied by the deprivation of the rights usually associated with being a national of a state. One of the deceits of the colonial system was to either deprive recognition of nationality to some categories of its subjects or to have various levels of rights accorded. The horrible scar that re-emerged in the heart of Europe in our days – the reality of ethnic cleansing – is quintessentially about the concept of national identity.

I remember watching the departure from Germany of a group of Croatian men in their early twenties and even younger heading off to take part in the Balkan conflict in the 1990s. These were young men who had been born, educated and had grown up in Germany and who knew geographic Croatia only as a place where they went on holiday, and who travelled on Yugoslav passports which made no mention of their Croat nation. The sense of nationality can run strong.

Paradoxically, a new awareness of globalisation is also accompanied by a strong sense of national and local identity, leading at times to tensions if the rights of national minorities within a state are not recognised.

One of the pillars of the Good Friday Agreement is the recognition of how much national identity means to the various parties who signed it. The agreement recognises the right of all persons born in Ireland 'to be part of the Irish nation', thus, all persons born in Northern Ireland can identify themselves culturally as either Irish or British and can be citizens of Ireland or Britain or both.

But it was not long before that formula had to be fine-tuned and reinterpreted through an amendment to the Irish Constitution. We live today in a world where human mobility is more and more common. The notion of nationality emerges in a new light in such a world. The debate about migration which is taking place the world over is also challenging governments to restrict the manner in which nationality can be acquired, especially through family bonds. Traditionally, in many legislative systems, a person acquired nationality through marriage and children of nationals would normally become nationals by descent, especially when born on the national territory. Fears about the abuse of immigration norms have led to a tightening of such positions. There is an implicit 'individualisation' of the person and a weakening of the sense of the family bond. The person can thus easily become seen as more akin to a useful economic commodity, pushing the desire for family reunification of migrants out of the picture.

Meanwhile, young Western people travel today in a manner that was inconceivable not so many years ago. They feel that they are citizens of the world. It is easy, however, to say that I am a 'citizen of the world' when I have a 'respectable' valid national passport in my pocket, knowing that when things go wrong I can turn for basic protection to the representatives of the state I am a national of.

Just think, however, of those who do not have a passport with such clear assurance of national identity. Think of those who are stateless because of historical conflicts; think of peoples whose nationality is not fully recognised around the world and have to rely on travel documents that raise questions at every international border or when stopped by any police officer. 'Everyone has the right to a nationality', the UDHR affirms. According to Article 24.3 of the International Covenant on Civil and Political Rights, 'Every child has the right to acquire a nationality.'

Nationality is a title for the exercise of basic rights within the state one is a national of. It is linked with the basic rights to vote and to participate in many aspects of national life. What is nationality? Is it something that comes from descent, in accordance with the principle of *jus sanguinis*, or is it linked with a bond with a territory, through being born in that territory (*jus soli*)?

Today's world makes it difficult to apply either in an absolute way. The definition of what constitutes nationality is traditionally attributed to national law and varies from state to state. International law comes into play where there are jurisdictional conflicts or where it is felt that national norms do not measure up to the level of protection required by international human rights instruments.

The borders of so many states do not correspond with the ethnic distribution of the population within them. Today, the very definition of democracy requires that we take account of the rights of minorities and various nationalities within the boundaries of a state. Simple rule by the majority is no longer a solid or sufficient principle to base democratic practice on. Democracy must foster the participation of minorities, including national minorities, present within a state.

Changing patterns of human mobility can result in anomalies within traditional practice regarding the recognition of nationality. Nationality can, for example, be used as an instrument for territorial expansion involving the concession on a large scale of citizenship to a particular group within a disputed territory or the withdrawal of recognition to particular nationalities and the application of discriminatory measures to a particular national group in a country.

People who do not belong to large national groups can easily become victims of abuse regarding their right to nationality. I think here of the ordeal of the Chagossian people expelled from the island of Diego Garcia to make room for a military base, who found themselves exiled from their own homeland with a very purpose-designed form of nationality which restricted their movement and above all would not allow them to return to their homeland.

More recently, there is also the curious phenomenon of the creation of an extra-territorial 'judicial' enclave in Guantánamo, where there are no nationals and attempts have been made to exclude the application of US domestic law to activities being carried out there in the name of the United States government.

While the authority of a government over its nationals relates primarily to their activities within the state, this is not always the case. It is useful to remember, for example, that numerous prescriptions of international humanitarian law regarding armed conflict and/or neutrality speak in terms of the actions and responsibilities of and towards 'nationals' and of the rights of 'nationals' to protection in terms of conflict.

Many laws today claim the right to prosecute certain activities committed by their nationals even outside their territory, a mechanism which is of special importance in combating the phenomenon of international trafficking and of sexual exploitation by nationals in other countries.

Globalisation has changed the way people interact in today's world. It has brought a greater awareness of interdependence and in many places, thank God, a strong reaction of international solidarity. But we still live in a world of nation states and the concept of nationality as a legal concept and as a human reality is as alive as ever.

The right to nationality belongs within the wider framework of human rights. Everyone has a right to a nationality and to the protection that this brings them. But everyone also has a right as a 'national' to live in an environment in which their rights are protected and fostered. Everyone has a right to see that the government of the state they are nationals of respects their rights and issues passports in the name of countries and regimes their nationals can be proud of.

women
AGAINST
violence
AGAINST
women

MARCH
AGAINST RAPE
TO TAKE PLACE ON
FRI.13th Oct.

STARTING AT 8.00pm

FROM MAIN GATE

AT STEPHENS GREEN

'Women against Violence against Women' march, Dublin, 1978

Crossmaglen British Army barracks, Northern Ireland, 1994

Moyross, Limerick, 2007

Ballymun Tower Block, Dublin, 1982

Finglas, Dublin, 1987

Protest against social welfare cuts, Dublin, 1986

Asylum seekers queue, Department of Foreign Affairs, Dublin 1997

Gama workers rally, Leinster House, Dublin, 2005

Temple Bar, Dublin, 2003

(1) MEN AND WOMEN OF FULL AGE, WITHOUT ANY LIMITATION DUE TO RACE, NATIONALITY OR RELIGION, HAVE THE RIGHT TO MARRY AND TO FOUND A FAMILY. THEY ARE ENTITLED TO EQUAL RIGHTS AS TO MARRIAGE, DURING MARRIAGE AND AT ITS DISSOLUTION.

(2) MARRIAGE SHALL BE ENTERED INTO ONLY WITH THE FREE AND FULL CONSENT OF THE INTENDING SPOUSES.

(3) THE FAMILY IS THE NATURAL AND FUNDAMENTAL GROUP UNIT OF SOCIETY AND IS ENTITLED TO PROTECTION BY SOCIETY AND THE STATE.

ARTICLE 16

Denise Charlton

CEO of the Immigrant Council of Ireland

Minister for Justice Dermot Ahern has ordered a review of immigration procedures after apologising before the High Court to a Somali woman over 'profound' system failures which resulted in her husband and three children being left in an Ethiopian camp for the last three years.

A 'profound systems failure is a succinct way of describing to the court what occurred, but it is entirely unsatisfactory. This is a gross and unacceptable act of maladministration ... What occurred in this case is not so much a systems failure but a consistent pattern of behaviour by the Department of Justice under the responsibility of a succession of Ministers for Justice'.

Shatter, *The Irish Times*, 26 July 2008

With over 130 million migrants and refugees worldwide, the proportion of families involved in or affected by migration is considerable. Globalisation has expanded the realm families live and work in and has created a new experience of family life for many. However, few migrants intend permanent or even long-term separation from loved ones, and so 'family reunification' is today one of the principal sources of migration in many countries. This is the term generally used to refer to the attempts to reunite with family members (however defined) in a country other than a person's country of origin. This can happen in different ways, depending on whether the application concerns family members who are living outside of Ireland or people who are already in Ireland at the time of seeking permission to stay, and on the status of the applicant. Irish immigration law and policy have yet to recognise the realities of family life and the rights of families.

The family's right to live together is protected by international human rights law. The Universal Declaration of Human Rights expressly recognises in Article 16 that: 'The family is the natural unit of society and is therefore entitled to protection from society and the State.' States have also recognised that children have a right to live with their parents and that the best interests of the child must be prioritised in this regard. The family is also defined and protected in this way by the Irish Constitution. Unfortunately, however, this is not reflected in how we in Ireland currently deal with families separated by migration. To date, enforceable rights to family reunification for people who come here to work, live or study have not been established, resulting in barriers to family life for many Irish and migrant families.

Over the past few decades, family reunification has been one of the principal sources of immigration in many countries, particularly in Europe. It has been estimated that about 30 per cent of the total international population of migrants are admitted to countries on family reunification grounds. This proportion is thought to be considerably higher in European countries. From both a fundamental rights and a pragmatic perspective, the importance of family reunification for migrants and receiving countries cannot be understated and this has been widely recognised at an international level. In particular, the European Union has accepted that family reunification measures are not only a way of bringing families back together, but that they are essential to facilitate integration and social inclusion in society.

In recognition of the principle of family unity and the need for the introduction of enforceable rights, there has been a right to family life for European Union citizens exercising their freedom of movement within the EU since 1968. In April 2004, EU member states adopted the Free Movement Directive (2004/38 EC), which replaced earlier directives with the same basic concept that EU citizens and their family members should be able to move between member states with their families on similar terms as nationals of a member state moving around or changing their place of residence in their own country.

However, Ireland's interpretation of this directive was so restrictive, acting as a major barrier to family life for EU citizens, that it was referred to the European Court of Justice (ECJ) by the High Court. The ECJ upheld the rights of EU citizens and their non-EU spouses who wished to live together in Ireland and found the state to be in breach of EU law. The court held that Irish regulations implementing the Free Movement Directive on the rights of EU citizens and their family members to move and reside freely within the EU was, in fact, contrary to the directive. At least 1,500 people have sought information and support from the Immigrant Council of Ireland (ICI) about these regulations over the past eighteen months. The restrictive nature of the Irish government's interpretation of the directive has caused enormous emotional and financial hardship for many families. It has resulted in situations where EU nationals already living and working in Ireland were told that their spouses could not join them here, effectively forcing a number of people to leave their jobs and return home or live without family members. The freedom of movement provision in the EC Treaty contains one of the most fundamental rights of EU nationals and their families, and the ICI is delighted to see the ECJ upholding this right so strongly. The ICI and others had been communicating the unlawful and unfair nature of the Irish regulations in various ways and it is regrettable that taking litigation as far as to the ECJ was necessary to affirm this fundamental right.

Despite the fact that international and domestic civil society organisations have recognised the importance of family unity, and despite the existence of international, domestic and constitutional laws, rights to family reunification have not been established in Irish law other than for recognised refugees and EU citizens.

The UDHR also states that 'men and women of full age, without any limitation due to race, nationality or religion, have the right to marry and to found a family'. Again, the Irish government resists this right in its present proposal to reform our legislative and policy framework for Immigration. The proposed legislation provides that a marriage contracted in Ireland between two people – one or both of whom is a foreign national – will be invalid in law unless they give three months' notice to the Minister for Justice, Equality and Law Reform of their intention to marry. Additionally, and even more problematically, the foreign national, or both of them, will have to be 'the holder of an entry permission issued for the purpose of the intended marriage or a residence permission (other than a protection application entry permission or a non-renewable residence permission)'. In other words, asylum-seekers and people on a non-renewable residence permit will not be permitted to marry in the state, even where they intend to marry an Irish or EU citizen. This is the first time that it has been proposed to use the institution of marriage as a form of immigration control.

There are many examples of our present and proposed immigration legislation that fail to respect the fundamental human right to 'marry and found a family'. It appears that this right is often dependent on country of origin, nationality, job and length of permission of residency. These barriers to family life are cited by those who use the ICI's services. Their experience highlights the barriers to family unity that currently exist and suggests that the legislative framework and the administrative system are in need of urgent reform. It is apparent that what is in place currently is a system that provides no statutory entitlement to family reunification for most people, and therefore no real access to the right to family life. Clear and transparent government policies or guidelines and criteria for decision-making are absent. Coupled with the largely discretionary nature of the present system, this results in anomalies and inconsistencies, unnecessary delays, discriminatory practices, high levels of refusals, and all with no independent appeals mechanism for redress.

In light of the significant contribution being made by migrants within Irish society, the government has an obligation to prioritise reform in this area. The ICI believes that a comprehensive and coherent policy in relation to family reunification should be developed and implemented as a matter of urgency and as part of the government's wider policy development and legislative reform in the field of immigration and integration in Ireland. Social policy development over the next few years must consider how best to manage and promote the integration of people who have arrived in Ireland in recent years. Family reunification is an important element in promoting integration and social cohesion and this issue needs to be explored further.

The absence of statutory rules governing the family reunification process, and in particular the failure to give immediate family members of Irish citizens a statutory right to family reunification, is a major gap in Irish law. The government has committed to developing regulations in relation to family life for migrants, although no timeframe was stipulated. However, the government has indicated that family reunification will not be addressed directly in primary legislation, but only in subsequent secondary legislation or practice guidelines. This proposal has been widely criticised and will not be subject to the same degree of scrutiny by the Houses of the Oireachtas. Therefore, members of the public and elected representatives will not have the same opportunity to examine and debate these rules before they are passed into law.

A legal right to family reunification for Irish citizens and all legal residents, set down in primary legislation, would provide immediate clarity of the system. The ICI implores the government to develop the new regulations and guidelines as a matter of urgency and to ensure they are underpinned by the principles and rights contained in the Universal Declaration of Human Rights.

(1) EVERYONE HAS THE RIGHT TO OWN PROPERTY ALONE AS WELL AS IN ASSOCIATION WITH OTHERS.

(2) NO ONE SHALL BE ARBITRARILY DEPRIVED OF HIS PROPERTY.

ARTICLE 17

Bob Jordan

Director of Threshold

The Irish Constitution of 1937 affirms the right to private property in two places: Article 40.3 and Article 43. This right to private property is counterbalanced by references to the common good and to social justice. There is, however, no mention of a right to housing.

Threshold is a housing charity and we help people who are homeless or live in vulnerable housing situations. We dealt with over 22,000 queries in 2007, including 674 people and households who were threatened with illegal eviction or were illegally evicted. Others needed our help to find housing or to negotiate on their behalf with their landlord.

Drawing on the experience of our clients, Threshold believes in a rights-based approach to housing. A right to housing would mean that Irish law makers would take account of this right when framing legislation. Irish courts would consider the right to housing when evaluating the constitutionality or legality of a statute. People who are tenants or those who are homeless could seek to exercise their right to housing when this has been overlooked by a public authority.

A right to housing consists of a number of elements, including accessibility to housing; security of tenure; affordability; location; and quality and cultural adequacy. A right to housing means that people, especially vulnerable people, can live in homes that have these qualities. If their accommodation falls short of these qualities, under a rights-based approach, they could seek to use the right to housing to acquire better housing.

As the right to housing is neither an enumerated nor an un-enumerated constitutional right, this has affected the framing of housing statutes in Ireland and, indeed, the jurisprudence of the Irish courts. Irish housing law would look very different if law-making involved balancing the right to private property with a right to housing. We would, for example, have real security of tenure for tenants. Instead, law-making is an exercise in balancing the right to property against the common good without any reference to a right to housing. This has placed people in need of housing or those with vulnerable tenure at a disadvantage. They cannot look to a right to housing in the Irish Constitution for support.

When assessing statutory provisions, the Irish superior courts have sought to balance the right to private property against the common good by using the doctrine of proportionality. Effectively, this doctrine assesses whether or not the impugned statutory provision represents an unjust attack on or interference with private property. There is no reference to the interests of people in need of housing, only the power of the state to intervene on their behalf.

Irish lawmakers have adapted to the constitutional emphasis on the right to private property by framing legislation which passes the test of unjust interference. This was the basis upon which Part V of the Planning and Development Act 2000 was upheld after it was referred to the Supreme Court by the president under Article 26 of the Constitution.

Part V compels private developers to set aside up to 20 per cent of developments above a certain size for social and affordable housing. This government initiative aimed to provide housing for people on local authority waiting lists and people who could not afford to buy housing on the private market. It also sought to promote 'social mix', with local authority tenants and private housing occupants living in the same developments rather than in segregated estates.

Part V was therefore designed to further the common good in two ways: by providing access to housing for vulnerable people and by promoting social cohesion. Despite this, the right to private property in the Constitution limited the government's ability to further the right to housing of vulnerable people and the wider interests of society. Part V was limited, as developers were entitled to full compensation and because of the relatively weak negotiating position of the local authorities vis-à-vis developers. This provision was further diluted by the subsequent Planning and Development (Amendment) Act 2002, which provided that developers could provide financial compensation in lieu of providing housing units. A financial payment is not an equivalent to the provision of a housing unit and the 2002 measure significantly dissipated the impact of Part V of the 2000 Act.

There has also been substantial change in Irish landlord and tenant law through the Residential Tenancies Act 2004. While Threshold is very supportive of this Act, the security of tenure it provides is limited because it only extends to four years and, during that time, the landlord has considerable scope to end the tonancy. The absence of a right to housing in the Irish Constitution can be seen to have contributed to this limitation. The opening sentence of the Long Title to the 2004 Act does not refer to providing for the needs of tenants with vulnerable tenures. Instead, it refers generally to the common good and says that, in accordance with the common good, the Act provides greater security of tenure for tenants.

Illegal Evictions in the Private Rented Sector

The fact that the right to private property has not been balanced by a right to housing has contributed to the practice of illegal evictions in the private rented sector.

An illegal eviction takes place when a landlord forcibly removes a tenant from their rented home. Illegal evictions involve a landlord changing the locks of a dwelling, with the tenant being physically ejected from a property, or having all their belongings destroyed. Threshold has helped tenants who have faced the hardship of sleeping in cars or sheds for the first few nights after an illegal eviction.

Illegal evictions are illegal because the landlord has not gone through the courts and because the sheriff did not put the necessary court order into effect. Anything other than a court-ordered action by the county or city sheriff is illegal.

Illegal evictions are not of recent provenance. Sadly, they have been a common occurrence in the private rented sector. They are common because a mindset has evolved amongst some landlords that illegal evictions are acts which can be justified. This mindset holds that if the relationship between landlord and tenant has broken down or if the tenant is in default, the landlord is entitled to regain possession of the property by whatever means necessary.

The Residential Tenancies Act 2004 established the Private Residential Tenancies Board (PRTB) so that landlords and tenants could resolve their disputes without going through the courts. This made it significantly easier for tenants to take cases against a landlord for a breach of landlord obligations without facing the jeopardy of legal costs. In 2007, Threshold represented tenants at over thirty illegal eviction cases before the PRTB and that figure trebled in 2008.

Illegal evictions contribute to making people homeless and are the ultimate breach of a person's right to housing. It is Threshold's experience that most landlords who evict their tenants illegally have not sought first to regain possession of their property lawfully. The establishment of the right to housing in Ireland would contribute to changing this mindset by creating a culture where arbitrarily depriving people of their home is not tolerated.

European Convention on Human Rights

While there is no constitutional right to housing, the European Convention on Human Rights (ECHR) provides a significant opportunity to develop a right to housing in Ireland.

Article 8 of the convention provides, *inter alia*, that everyone has the right to respect for their home. The convention is incorporated into Irish law at a sub-constitutional level through the European Convention on Human Rights Act 2003. Article 8 has already benefited local authority tenants seeking to challenge eviction notices initiated under section 62 of the Housing Act 1966.

This section provides that a district court can grant a warrant of possession where the tenancy has been terminated by a notice to quit. In a recent case, *Donegan vs. Dublin City Council*, Ms Justice Laffoy concluded that section 62 did not comply with Article 8 of the convention because it did not provide sufficient safeguards to a person's right to housing. Specifically, the local authority did not allow an independent review of the facts that had led to the service of a notice to quit.

Threshold considers this to be an important step forward for local authority tenants. As a result of this High Court decision, Threshold believes that the Housing Act 1966 must be amended to allow tenants to refer a dispute to an independent review body when they have been served with a notice to quit. This is the safeguard afforded to tenants under Article 8 of the ECHR. Such an amendment would enable local authorities to pursue tenants who are in breach of the conditions of their tenancy while complying with the rights protected by the convention.

The ECHR offers an opportunity to develop a right to housing in Ireland and decisions like the *Donegan* case represent progress on the principles put forward by the UDHR sixty years ago. However, the ECHR is limited to respecting the right to a home and will not contribute to promoting other aspects of the right to housing, such as access to housing and affordability. For these issues to be addressed, a right to housing informed by Article 17 of the UDHR, but grounded in a domestic legal instrument is necessary.

EVERYONE HAS THE RIGHT TO FREEDOM OF THOUGHT, CONSCIENCE AND RELIGION; THIS RIGHT INCLUDES FREEDOM TO CHANGE HIS RELIGION OR BELIEF, AND FREEDOM, EITHER ALONE OR IN COMMUNITY WITH OTHERS AND IN PUBLIC OR PRIVATE, TO MANIFEST HIS RELIGION OR BELIEF IN TEACHING, PRACTICE, WORSHIP AND OBSERVANCE.

ARTICLE 18

Dr Katherine Zappone

Public Policy Research Consultant and member of the Irish Human Rights Commission

'Freedom of Thought, Conscience and Religion': Capital for Social Change in Ireland

How can Article 18 of the 1948 Universal Declaration of Human Rights be a living resource for people in Ireland in the twenty-first century? Does this article contain a potency of meaning – that is, enough meaning – to motivate citizens, residents and public leaders towards private and public action that will contribute to a social cohesion strong enough to create a place of well-being for everyone here? Perhaps we could say that this should be the function of the entire declaration, that all articles taken together ought to offer a rich resource to guide our private action, public policies, laws and growth as a society. My task, however, is to focus on an article considered to be one of the most fundamental human rights within the international legal order, and one that has featured in several subsequent human rights conventions and declarations, most significantly within the International Covenant on Civil and Political Rights 1966 (ICCPR) (Article 18), the UN Declaration on the Elimination of All Forms of Intolerance and Discrimination Based on Religion or Belief 1981, and the European Convention on Human Rights 1950 (Article 9 as 'incorporated' into Irish law by the ECHR Act 2003).

Throughout this evolution of international debate and consensus, the focus has largely been on the human right to freedom of religion, as distinct from the freedom of thought or conscience or, indeed, protection of the right not to ascribe to any religion. While the latter elements are not excluded, a conventional view of Article 18 centres on how it calls on the state and its citizens to tolerate religious diversity and to ensure that no one suffers discrimination because of her or his religious identity. So I wish to begin with a brief reflection on religion in light of my experience as a theologian and as a human rights advocate. This will lead to a less conventional view of the application of this article's relevance for Ireland today.

For any religion to avoid what is popularly known as 'funda-mentalism', it ought to contain structures of authority and leadership that do not exclude any human being by virtue of her or his identity. For example, there are religious traditions at this current juncture in history that exclude women and people with minority sexual identities from organisational positions of articulating the religion's meaning and relevance for the world. Why should the state protect the toleration of religious diversity if diversity is not protected within religion?

Secondly, similar to the legal philosophy that foundational legal documents (such as constitutions or international conventions) ought to be interpreted in light of the changing social context so that they maintain ethical relevance, I suggest that the interpretation of sacred texts, religious traditions, doctrines, practices and forms of worship ought to engage with current social realities and be open to changing meaning and teaching in light of that engagement. Where does the truth of what it means to live a good and human life reside? How can the present social context of ordinary lives being lived reveal and inform what is meant by the good life? A religion stays alive and avoids rigid fundamentalism if its leaders and believers apply the ongoing discipline of interpreting the truths of the past in light of the truths of the present.

A third observation that surfaces from the dialogue between theological and human rights practice is this: while a person's religion is a deeply personal matter, it ought to prompt responsibility for a just and equal society. Perhaps I betray here my own religion of origin, namely, the Roman Catholic variety of

Christianity, and the centrality of its tenet: 'Love God with your whole heart, and love your neighbour as yourself.'

A religious world view, however, regardless of its teachings, provides the believer or practitioner with a pathway towards the experience of the divine, or the ground of being, or that which is beyond the human. For what purpose, though? Surely it must have something to do with coming to a better sense and awareness of what conditions in society are needed so that the beauty and graciousness of human dignity and freedom are respected and allowed to unfold. If this is so, the right to freedom of religion moves from the realm of 'tolerating diversity' and protecting against discrimination towards the arena of capital for positive social change.

While a striking characteristic of the Ireland of the past was its religious homogenity with the dominance of Roman Catholicism, present-day Ireland manifests significant growth in religious diversity. *Census 2006* records a population of 4,239,848, whereby 86.8 per cent claim Roman Catholic identity (as contrasted with 93 per cent in 1981), 5.5 per cent register as non-Catholic Christians, of which the Orthodox is the fastest-growing group. There is a doubling of Hindus since 2002 (now at 6,082), a 150 per cent increase of Apostolic and Pentacostals, a slight increase in the Jewish population (standing at 1,930), and 0.5 per cent of people in Ireland are Muslim (32,539). There was an increase, to 4.4 per cent of the population, of those who recorded that they do not have any religious affiliation, and that right is also protected by the Universal Declaration. I wish to suggest that such an increasing heterogenity of religious membership provides a critical opportunity for the children and young people of Ireland to be educated in a way that enables them to engage seriously with how the sacred stories, ethics and customs of their religious communities support the fostering of justice, freedom and equality with those of other religious and philosophic world views.

What I am proposing is this: that the state finds innovative ways to protect this newly emerging religious diversity, particularly in its system of education. This would provide a unique opportunity for young people to learn about difference in religious meaning, values and lifestyles, preferably alongside those who are different from them.

A pressing challenge for education today is to create literacy and fluency in understanding religious diversity. Such an education in, and appreciation of, difference can do a number of things for our young citizens and residents. First, it can assist them to develop a more critical perspective about their own religious identity. They will be more likely to question thoughtfully traditional or contemporary beliefs, thereby owning them for themselves or indeed proposing changes to them from within their community of practice, in light of the dialogue with difference. Second, as interreligious or multireligious dialogue is promoted within schools, not simply in theory but through the presence and participation by those of differing traditions or outlooks, space can be created to debate together the implications of differing religious and ethical perspectives on the social, family and economic policies and laws of the country. Imagine if our future politicians, lawyers, civil servants, businesswomen and men, teachers, doctors, tradesmen or women, nurses and religious and civic leaders had this kind of educational experience to bring to bear on their voting practices, design and implementation of law and public policy? Third, such an educational effort to promote the relevance of religions and ethics to public life – *within* an environment of respect for 'freedom of thought, conscience and religion' – would be more likely to support freedom of thought *within* religion as well as maximise the potential of diverse ethical visions to drive social change in Ireland.

There are promising signs on the horizon for this kind of transformative change. The Department of Education and Science recognises the governance challenges for future primary schools. With projections of an additional 100,000 pupils entering the educational system within the next decade – many of whom will come from newly immigrated families – the state is intensely involved with its education partners to develop new models of school patronage and provision in order to meet the full range of diverse community needs. A new model of community national school (or state-run primary school) is being piloted in two Dublin settings. These schools will be intentionally characterised by an ethos of inclusion, equality and harmony of multifaith and non-faith perspectives, with the state committed to providing religious education within the school curriculum in a way that acknowledges religious diversity. Educate Together, established in 1984 to provide multidenominational primary schools – with the philosophy that 'children of all social, cultural and religious backgrounds have a right to an education that respects their individual identity whilst exploring the different values and traditions of the world in which we live' – now provides patronage to fifty-six primary schools.

The Irish Catholic Church (holding 92 per cent patronage of primary schools) has argued for greater plurality of provision to respond effectively to the changing needs of Irish society. The Catholic Archbishop of Dublin, Dr Diarmuid Martin, is on record in his support of expanding the role of other patronage models, and he also maintains that Catholic schools must provide a tolerant religious environment for those of other backgrounds. St Patrick's College Drumcondra, one of the Colleges of Education for Irish primary school teachers, conducts innovative modules in 'Religious Education and Diversity' and 'Thinking and Teaching in Different School Contexts'.

Sixty years on, the Universal Declaration's aspiration of freedom in thought, conscience and religion may be more relevant in Ireland now than ever before. My hope is that this foundational human right – allowed to flourish in all its diversity – will bring about more peace, justice and equality than exists in Ireland today.

EVERYONE HAS THE RIGHT TO FREEDOM OF OPINION AND EXPRESSION; THIS RIGHT INCLUDES FREEDOM TO HOLD OPINIONS WITHOUT INTERFERENCE AND TO SEEK, RECEIVE AND IMPART INFORMATION AND IDEAS THROUGH ANY MEDIA AND REGARDLESS OF FRONTIERS.

ARTICLE 19

Dearbhail McDonald

Legal Editor of the *Irish Independent*

Reflecting on her experience as a banned author, Edna O'Brien observed that censorship is rooted in fear: 'Fear of knowledge. Fear of communicating our desires, our secrets, our stream of consciousness.' The Irish Censorship Board banned almost all of her fiction published during the 1960s; many of her books were burned in church grounds and one woman feared she was possessed by the devil after reading *Girls in their Married Bliss*.

Irish history is littered with icons silenced or exiled under official and unofficial censorship regimes and no aspect of Irish life escaped the scythe of the censors. Freedom of expression in art, music, film, literature and politics was suppressed and distorted in the name of independence, morality, Church and state. Even the human need to confront essential truths, such as war, love and sexuality, were repressed by state and Church puritans, supported by a blind and willing citizenry, all products of the times they lived in. For a time, censorship was a badge of honour worn by Irish artists who joined Marcel Proust, Ernest Hemingway, Dylan Thomas and Vladimir Nabokov on the 'indecent and obscene' roll call of shame. It seems comical now that Walt Disney's *Fantasia* was one of 11,000 films that were banned, or that cinemagoers never got to see Rhett Butler and Scarlett O'Hara's famous kiss in *Gone with the Wind*. Scandalous too that the late John McGahern was fired from his job as a teacher and forced to emigrate because his banned novel, *The Dark*, contained the word 'fuck' on the first page and described a boy masturbating.

The rebranding of the Irish Film Censor's Office to the Irish Film Classification Office marked the dismantling of the final draconian apparatus of state censorship, but that does not mean that our primal instinct for secrecy is a relic of the past. Think, for example, of the lasting impact of the section 31 broadcasting ban or the epic struggle for abortion information. Think of the damage caused by the cover-up of the clerical sex and institutional abuse scandals and the unknown effects of the erosion of the Freedom of Information Acts. Think of the editing, two years ago, of Trócaire's Lenten campaign advertisement because it was deemed political and the government's 'rationalisation' spree that slashed the budgets of the Equality Authority and the Irish Human Rights

Commission in 2008. These bodies were necessarily critical of aspects of government policy and their budgetary cuts confirm what we know about certain acts of censorship: the state does not need statutes to silence its detractors.

Murder is the ultimate act of censorship. Learning about journalists who have been killed – more than 700 worldwide in the past sixteen years – makes me realise how fortunate I am to be working as a reporter in a progressive, peaceful democracy. The vast majority of Irish media professionals take it for granted that they are free to produce news and hold opinions without the fear of persecution, imprisonment or being 'disappeared'. We are aware that in foreign war zones, despotic regimes and even in some democracies, our colleagues risk their lives with every sentence they write and every image they capture. Ireland regularly tops various world press freedom indices, whose authors praise our lack of recorded censorship, threats, intimidation and physical reprisals.

The Irish Constitution of 1937, the European Convention of Human Rights and the UN Declaration of Human Rights together provide a legal and moral framework that bolsters the virtues of a free press. Irish journalists are, for the most part, free to publish without fearing for our livelihoods or our lives. We publish news that informs, news that sickens and outrages, news that entertains and news that has no value at all.

We publish news that is in the public interest and news that the public are interested in but have no real business knowing at all. We hold public figures and celebrities to account and are allowed to serve as the permanent opposition by publishing material that questions, condemns and, where necessary, derides the powers that be.

Yet censorship, a creature of degree as much as of kind, still holds us in its grip. Two journalists, Veronica Guerin of the *Sunday Independent* and Martin O'Hagan of the *Sunday World*, have been murdered in recent years because of their investigations.

In Northern Ireland, journalists still face threats because of their reporting; in the Republic, one journalist lives under constant garda protection. Two, possibly three, journalists, including Geraldine Kennedy, editor of *The Irish Times*, face the prospect of prison for refusing to reveal their sources, following controversial leaks arising from the work of tribunals of inquiry.

Even journalists, a belligerent and self-important bunch at the best of times, acknowledge that the right to freedom of expression is not absolute. We are not above the law. We realise that there are times when secrecy is justified. We collude in conspiracies of silence, by non-publication, when it is acknowledged that certain issues need to be cloaked by confidentiality. We accept there are times when information cannot be revealed because it is not in the public interest to do so.

The problem, of course, is that the public interest, much like privacy, is virtually impossible to define. There is also the vexed question of who actually gets to define the public interest. Should it be the government, power brokers and vested interests who stand to gain most from a culture of non-disclosure? Should it be unelected judges? Should it be the media, whose independence is compromised, with increasing ferocity, by the pursuit of profit? Or should the people decide what is best for us?

In my experience as a reporter, Irish officialdom is obsessed with secrecy. The default position is to say nothing at all or as little as possible. It irritates and even angers certain state agencies when journalists or members of the public seek even the most basic, non-controversial information about their activities and decision-making processes, never mind the juicy, significant stuff.

At the same time, journalists have been subjected to an information revolution with the proliferation of 'spin' that envelops government activity and private enterprise. We are bombarded daily with often meaningless, but carefully constructed, information packages that rarely contain the crucial or controversial information that the public actually needs.

So, reporters resort to covert, sometimes illegal, means: befriending whistleblowers, targeting insiders, surveillance, trespass, breaches of privacy and the like. Often, freedom of expression demands such strategies, even when our laws do not permit them. Journalists are also seduced by off-the-record briefings that make us feel important and trusted, but which reveal little or, worse, place us in the deplorable position of acting as a conduit between a vested interest and the public to relay a specific or malevolent agenda. The legal machinery of censorship is also well entrenched in Irish journalism practice. Government and other reports are withheld for unspecified 'legal reasons' and cannot be published because there will be 'consequences'.

Day in, day out, journalists' copy is 'pre-pubbed', where teams of lawyers sift through stories to seek out and destroy any potentially lethal text. This legalling process acts as a welcome cushion against the chilling effects of our archaic defamation laws but is, in a manner of speaking, censorship. Much of what is 'spiked' (removed or revised) is, in fact, publishable, but editors err on the side of caution lest they run the risk of erratic compensation awards and the eye-watering legal costs that accompany a contested libel action.

And just as we are about to finally reform our defamation regime, Ireland faces the threat of a regressive privacy law that, if enacted in its current form, will stymie investigative journalism and herald a new era of censorship to be exploited by those wealthy or powerful enough to hide their transgressions.

It would be deceitful, silly even, to deny that external, commercial, editorial and political pressures do not play their part in the everyday self-censorship that is practised by journalists. They do. And the pressure to appease executives, advertisers, senior colleagues and sources you are close to is tangible and very real. In an era of mass-media ownership, moguls and 'views papers', journalists instinctively know what works and what does not, what will make the page and what will end up on the cutting floor.

I challenge any journalistic colleague to deny the existence of those realities that can serve to test our integrity and threaten to compromise our fundamental duty to search for the truth, to make common property that information which we manage (sometimes with difficulty) to obtain. Journalists must stand firm against these pressures and remind ourselves that the intelligence we receive is not ours: it is the property of the public we serve. We cannot filter or shut out the light we shine on the dark corners of our human experience.

I believe that self-censorship by journalists, intended or subconscious, is the enemy of truth and perhaps the greatest risk to freedom of expression and opinion in our time.

Despite the freedoms we enjoy sixty years after the UDHR, there is an ever-constant need for vigilance against all forms of censorship. As Edna O'Brien warned: 'Banning is only the tip of the iceberg. Keeping our psyches closed is the main bogey.'

(1) EVERYONE HAS THE RIGHT TO FREEDOM OF PEACEFUL ASSEMBLY AND ASSOCIATION.

(2) NO ONE MAY BE COMPELLED TO BELONG TO AN ASSOCIATION.

ARTICLE 20

Ronnie Fay

Director of Pavee Point Travellers' Centre

Freedom of assembly and association has played a central role in vindicating the rights of minorities in Ireland, as it has done in many other countries. It immediately evokes images of the struggle to realise civil rights in Northern Ireland in the 1960s, the work of the trade union movement to vindicate the rights of workers (particularly those in low-paid and insecure employment) and the work of those in non-governmental bodies who have fought for equality, sometimes with the support of government but some-times working against apathy or hostility.

Peaceful assembly and association, as practised through community development, have also been key features of the struggle to vindicate the rights of the Traveller community in Ireland. When Pavee Point Travellers' Centre was established in 1985, the newspapers were full of evocative photographs of nuns, Travellers and community workers being dragged away from the paths of bulldozers as the construction of the Tallaght bypass made scores of Traveller families homeless, with no regard to the fact that most had lived in the Tallaght area for decades, long before the peripheral estates of West Tallaght were completed in the early 1980s.

The temporary solution of the local authority to this homelessness crisis, like that of many other local authorities before them, was to construct a huge temporary halting site, St Maelruain's, which was overcrowded with forty Traveller families, enclosed by earthen ditches that were a haven for rats, and lacking any facilities beyond the very basic.

Subsequent events in Tallaght showed that those who had protested in 1985 were right to be concerned. The 'temporary' halting site of St Maelruain's was to exist for a further fifteen years. Thankfully, it was closed, but a further huge temporary site, Lynch's Lane, still remains in Clondalkin some thirty years after it was first built and provides continuing problems for Travellers and local residents.

In October 2004, the right to peaceful assembly and association was again tested by Travellers' opposition to a concrete barrier located at Ratoath Road and Dunsink Lane in the Finglas area of

Dublin. Without warning and circumventing long-established channels of communications, Dublin City Council erected the barrier, which forced Travellers living in the area to make a very long detour to get to shops, local schools and other facilities.

Traveller representatives protested by mounting a peaceful picket and were arrested on foot of pressure from the council. The local gardaí, who had built up good relations with Travellers in the area over many years, carried out the arrests reluctantly.

The incident and the arrests caused disturbances in the area by a small number of angry Travellers. The issue was finally resolved, as it should have been in the first instance, by peaceful negotiation between Traveller groups, the gardaí and the council. Speaking at the time, Martin Collins, Assistant Director of Pavee Point and one of those arrested, said: 'We all need to learn from this experience. An ounce of prevention is worth a pound of intervention. This barrier should never have been erected. It has increased hostility between Travellers and the majority population and fuelled negative media coverage on Traveller issues. We hope the state sector learns from this experience that you must engage with Travellers in issues that affect our lives.'

The right to peaceful assembly and association was again tested by the protests held to highlight the conditions experienced by the Roma families on an M50 roundabout in the summer of 2007.

Pavee Point was initially contacted by members of An Garda Síochána who were concerned in the early summer about Roma families living rough in north County Dublin. The statutory agencies that had been contacted felt they could not intervene because of instructions from the Department of Justice, Equality and Law Reform. The department was concerned that providing humanitarian support would increase Roma migration to Ireland and that Ireland would somehow be seen as a 'soft spot'. Pavee Point and Roma Support Group Ireland were concerned that while the state had a legitimate right to protect its borders, this right should not be exercised at the expense of human life. There was an immediate humanitarian duty of care to the Roma men, women and children, including infants.

The plight of the Roma attracted considerable media attention when one extended family, the Rostas, encamped on a roundabout in the middle of a major motorway junction on the M50 near Ballymun. The extended family ranged in age from a six-week-old baby, who was born in Ireland, to a sixty-year-old grandmother. They lived in old two-person tents and makeshift shelters constructed from pieces of plastic, old election posters and debris they had collected from nearby skips. Conditions in the makeshift camp deteriorated rapidly in the heavy summer rain of 2007. Despite the obvious hazards arising from the encampment to the many children and passing motorists, the government stuck rigidly to its position of non-intervention.

Pavee Point and other organisations, including the National Consultative Committee on Racism and Interculturalism (NCCRI), came under heavy criticism from the Department of Justice, Equality and Law Reform at the time. At one stage, Pavee Point was even told that it could lose its public funding as a result of its efforts to highlight the humanitarian problems experienced by the M50 Roma.

The Roma received some support from the general public donating food and clothes to the families. Most of the support came from the Traveller community living in and around the area, who as well as providing moral support, donated food, clothing, blankets and delivered cooked hot meals. Crosscare, the Catholic charity, also provided humanitarian support during this crisis.

The Roma family on the M50 repeatedly voiced the concern that they did not want to return to Romania because of the conditions in their place of origin, Tileagd in the Bihor region. Many Roma families in this part of Romania were living in inadequate accommodation which often comprised of very basic houses without electricity, heating or running water. They did not receive any social welfare or other payments in Romania apart from child benefit, which is equivalent to two days' food per month. The Roma survived by collecting rubbish and scrap, recycling glass and metals and occasionally doing casual work in agriculture or labouring. When times were really bad, the families were forced to eat from rubbish bins and tips. They felt that they had no chance of improving their living circumstances and opportunities in Romania and, as parents, they wanted the best future for their children.

Under pressure from within Ireland, and in response to considerable media pressure, the Irish authorities eventually did intervene and assisted the Roma families to return to Romania.

While Pavee Point has and continues to enjoy positive relations and support from government bodies, including the Department of Justice, Equality and Law Reform, it is also clear that, at critical times, this relationship has been severely strained, testing its exercise of the right to assembly and association. The Irish government continues to fund important initiatives, including the most recent Traveller Focus Week held in December 2008.

However, in the past year it has been evident that government is sending out an increasingly strong message to all NGOs involved in rights work, not just those working with Travellers. The core of the message is that the role of NGOs is to provide services and not to advocate for people's rights or disagree with the government. This is a worrying trend and one that is contrary to the principles of free assembly and association which are so integral to our history and, indeed, were central to the struggle for national independence.

Barack Obama, President of the United States, recently stated: 'I will always be honest with you about the challenges we face. I will listen to you, especially when we disagree. And, above all, I will ask you to join in the work of remaking this nation.' These are words with a global import and resonance and should inform how governments perceive those who are advocating for change, inclusion and improvement in the rights of our most marginalised communities.

(1) EVERYONE HAS THE RIGHT TO TAKE PART IN THE GOVERNMENT OF HIS COUNTRY, DIRECTLY OR THROUGH FREELY CHOSEN REPRESENTATIVES.

(2) EVERYONE HAS THE RIGHT OF EQUAL ACCESS TO PUBLIC SERVICE IN HIS COUNTRY.

(3) THE WILL OF THE PEOPLE SHALL BE THE BASIS OF THE AUTHORITY OF GOVERNMENT; THIS WILL SHALL BE EXPRESSED IN PERIODIC AND GENUINE ELECTIONS WHICH SHALL BE BY UNIVERSAL AND EQUAL SUFFRAGE AND SHALL BE HELD BY SECRET VOTE OR BY EQUIVALENT FREE VOTING PROCEDURES.

ARTICLE 21

Joanna McMinn

Former Director of the National Women's Council of Ireland (NWCI)

Introduction

I propose to consider, from an international perspective, what Article 21 of the Universal Declaration of Human Rights (UDHR) means for women in Ireland, and their current low level of participation in decision-making in this country. I will also address what strategies are being used elsewhere, and what would work in Ireland, to redress current inequalities and to give real and substantive meaning to the text of Article 21 of the UHDR.

Article 21 could be read as a negative right or a freedom from interference in the sense that you cannot prevent someone going forward for election. No one would deny that, currently, women have the same equal or formal right as men to go forward for election to political parties or as independent candidates if they wish to participate in government and public service. Women do, of course, enjoy universal suffrage in which their right to vote is not restricted by race, gender, belief or social status, a right that was fought for and won by suffragists and suffragettes in the early twentieth century.

Article 21 could also be approached as a positive right, and implemented in an active or purposive way, to address the current disconnect between the theory of universal suffrage and the reality of women's current under-representation among those who make high-level decisions in government and public service.

International Perspective

The average proportion worldwide of women members of single or lower chamber legislatures is just 18 per cent, with major regional differences. Less than 10 per cent of cabinet members and just

20 per cent of lower-ranking government ministers globally are female, and only thirty-nine nation states have ever selected a woman as prime minister or president.

Twenty-one countries have over 30 per cent representation – the minimum percentage deemed necessary for women to exert meaningful influence on politics – including countries in Sub-Saharan Africa, Latin America and the Caribbean, as well as in industrialised countries. This illustrates the fact that women's representation is not linked to whether a country is rich or poor. The United States has 16.8 per cent women representatives and Japan has 9 per cent, while the country with the highest representation, Rwanda, has 48.8 per cent women representatives and Cuba has 43 per cent.

Among European countries, Spain and Belgium have shown the most remarkable progress; in the period from 1995 to 2008, Spain's level of representation of women rose from 16 per cent to 36 per cent and Belgium's from 12 per cent to 35 per cent. Austria, Denmark, Finland, the Netherlands, Norway and Sweden have all maintained higher than average levels in that period; in 2008, all had over 30 per cent women representatives in their national parliaments. The average proportion in the European Union of women members of parliament (single/lower house) rose from 16 per cent in 1997 to 24 per cent in 2007. In a further seven EU countries, women account for less than 15 per cent of members of parliament – the Czech Republic, Cyprus, Hungary, Malta, Romania, Slovenia and, of course, Ireland.

While no national parliament has full equality in the number of seats held by women and men, Ireland is particularly under-represented. In 2008, it ranked eighty-sixth out of 192 countries in terms of the percentage of women holding office in the lower, or single, house of the national parliamentary body. Disappointingly, and despite calls for change, the percentage of women in Ireland's lower house, Dáil Éireann, has remained static at 13 per cent since 1995.

Women's participation in government and public services matters. Currently, we have a democratic deficit in Ireland, where the serious under-representation of women in decision-making perpetuates gender inequality and diminishes the human rights of women. The NWCI has long argued for a more balanced group of representatives, which we believe would lead to better decision-making and political priorities that more closely reflect the concerns of the full range of voters. Key issues of concern to women include poverty alleviation, pensions, reproductive rights, childcare and gender-related violence. In particular, combating violence against women is an area in which women legislators have made their presence felt in all regions of the world. The UN committee that responds to the Irish government's report on progress in implementing the Convention on the Elimination of All Forms of Discrimination Against Women (CEDAW) has specifically called on the government to take action on these areas. The CEDAW committee has also called on the Irish government 'to take sustained measures to increase the [parliamentary] representation of women, including temporary special measures; and to form a parliamentary committee to research the root causes of delay in this area'.

Positive Action

International evidence has shown that the only way to increase the number of women in parliament significantly is to use positive action measures. The question is what kind of positive action measures are most effective in different electoral systems and what would be the most effective approach in the Irish context?

Most of the countries that have achieved critical mass have an electoral system based on proportional representation with some form of quota system to proactively reduce the obstacles to women entering politics at national level. In many of the Nordic countries, which have among the highest political representation of women in the world, political parties have explicitly adopted quotas guaranteeing that 40–50 per cent of a party's candidates list are women. While the Nordic experience provides evidence that legislative gender quotas can help to bring about real and rapid change, the use of quotas remains controversial.

Belgium's improvement in the parliamentary gender balance over the past ten years (from 12 per cent to 35 per cent women) was a direct result of positive intervention by the government through legislation enforcing parity amongst candidates and equal visibility on ballot papers – for example, the first two names on the list should not be of the same sex.

Spain's progress over the same period (from 16 per cent to 36 per cent) has been brought about by political will, demonstrated by the introduction of legislation in 2006 imposing the so-called '40 per cent rule'. This prohibits men or women from making up more than 60 per cent of the candidates of any political party that contests national or local elections. The new Spanish cabinet, sworn in by the socialist Prime Minister José Luis Rodríguez-Zapatero in April 2008, has nine women alongside eight men, demonstrating a remarkable political leadership. 'I am not only an anti-machoist, I am a feminist,' Mr Zapatero once said. 'The most unfair domination is that of one half of humanity over the other. The more equality women have, the more civilised and tolerant society will be.'

In Scandinavia, where there is no legislative demand for high representation of women, progress is attributed to the sustained pressure from women's groups within political parties and the women's movement in general to increase the number of women candidates and those with a chance of actually winning. The Scandinavian experience demonstrates that the promotion of equality in general can lead to the emergence of a political culture that enables women, once elected, to operate effectively and promote further increases in the numbers of women parliamentarians.

The Way Forward in Ireland

The Irish government's statement of priorities in relation to the advancement of women in Irish society for the period 2007–2016 is enshrined in the National Women's Strategy (NWS), whose vision is of 'an Ireland where all women enjoy equality with men and can achieve their full potential, while enjoying a safe and fulfilling life'. The NWS contains the Irish government's targets on actions to increase the number of women in decision-making positions in Ireland. It also places responsibility on the political parties to develop action plans aimed at increasing the number of female candidates in general elections so that there will be a significant increase in the representation of women in all future elections to local authorities, the Dáil, Seanad and European Parliament.

Political parties in Ireland are critical in bringing about change because they determine, as gatekeepers, who gets on the candidate list. Political parties have been proactive in other countries in creating a list system that ensures gender balance on lists of political candidates; Irish political parties can do, and some have done, the same. However, the entry level into political parties is often at local level. Participation in decision-making at local level in Ireland reflects a low representation of women despite the fact that women's participation in community and voluntary activities and in seeking to influence policies and voice their concerns is at a high level. Some of the barriers that have been identified for women gaining entry to political representation at local level include financial obstacles, lower levels of confidence, education, training and capacity-building, caring responsibilities and childcare, structural and institutional discrimination, and the low value attributed to women's community work (*Every Step of the Way: Women Accessing Power in Dublin City*, Dublin City Council Working Group, International Women's Day, 8 March 2008).

There is clearly a strong resistance to change and, unless there is a dramatic emergence of political will, women's groups in political parties and the women's movement in general will need to continue to lobby and sustain the pressure for greater equality within Irish society.

On the sixtieth anniversary of the Universal Declaration of Human Rights, Ireland's commitment to full equality for men and women can be measured by the extent to which the state is willing to invest in electoral reform to make Article 21 a reality that matches a noble rhetoric.

EVERYONE, AS A MEMBER OF SOCIETY, HAS THE RIGHT TO SOCIAL SECURITY AND IS ENTITLED TO REALISATION, THROUGH NATIONAL EFFORT AND INTERNATIONAL CO-OPERATION AND IN ACCORDANCE WITH THE ORGANISATION AND RESOURCES OF EACH STATE, OF THE ECONOMIC, SOCIAL AND CULTURAL RIGHTS INDISPENSABLE FOR HIS DIGNITY AND THE FREE DEVELOPMENT OF HIS PERSONALITY.

ARTICLE 22

Fr Seán Healy

Director of CORI Justice

The Current Situation

At a moment of major change both globally and locally, Article 22 of the Universal Declaration of Human Rights is of particular relevance to Ireland. The challenges currently facing policy-makers, and society in general, provide an opportunity to reflect on the kind of society Irish people would like to live in, to identify what is required if such a society is to be developed and to check if the resources that a prosperous Ireland has accumulated are being used to best effect to achieve this kind of desirable future.

Despite a decade and a half of prosperity, Ireland finds itself with serious deficits in infrastructure (e.g. public transport, broadband) and in social services (e.g. education, health, social welfare) that could and should have been addressed effectively by now. Likewise, the environment is at risk and under increasing threat.

Many good developments resulted from the economic growth of the Celtic Tiger years, but they have been paralleled by closely linked negative developments or failures. While per capita income has grown dramatically, in 2008, 17 per cent of the population still lived in poverty with incomes below €11,400 a year for a single person and €26,400 for a household of four. Likewise, the number of jobs almost doubled over this period and unemployment fell dramatically. However, while house-building reached record levels, the waiting lists for social housing were not reduced significantly. Many other examples could be cited. Public policy has failed to address effectively the huge challenges posed by these developments in the new Ireland.

A Question of Development Models

The development model followed was deeply flawed. A new approach is needed if Irish people are to achieve a real improvement in their well-being in the years immediately ahead. A development model that focuses almost exclusively on economic growth as the key to increasing people's well-being is doomed to failure. Economic development and social development are complementary and should be given equal priority. If this had been done during the Celtic Tiger years, we would now have the infrastructure and social services required to ensure that every person in Ireland was capable of living life with dignity.

A Broader Understanding of Rights

Civil, political, social, economic and cultural rights and obligations characterise, to varying degrees, membership in all economically developed societies. Civil and political rights relating to liberty of the person and property rights, and the right to vote and to organise or associate freely, have a long history. They date from the eighteenth and nineteenth centuries in most Western European countries, although their universal application has come about much later in all countries. While civil and political rights and obligations are now generally uncontested in Western European countries, there is less agreement on social, economic and cultural rights and obligations.

Social and economic rights and obligations are far more recent in origin than civil and political rights; their development roughly parallels the development of the range of social and economic policies broadly identified as the welfare state. Noteworthy amongst these policies are health and education, social services, income maintenance and recognition that the state has an obligation to act in the event of market failure as reflected, for example, in mass unemployment.

The recognition of cultural rights is even more recent. The scope and quality of social, economic and cultural rights vary considerably across countries and are contested to different degrees in most countries. Whereas equality in civil and political rights implies treating everyone the same (consistent with 'equality of opportunity'), equality in social, economic and cultural rights may imply recognising differences associated with particular conditions or statuses that exclude individuals from the mainstream and framing policy accordingly. Consequently, some of these rights which require treating 'difference' differently may enjoy less public support than the more straightforward civil and political rights and those social rights that have a potentially more universal uptake, such as education up to the end of the second cycle.

Rights and Obligations

Obligations associated with social, economic and cultural rights are less clearly defined than obligations associated with civil and political rights. Rights are not independent of one another; for example, the exercise of civil or political rights may be dependent on access to economic, social and cultural rights. It is important to bear in mind that rights that are universal in principle may be limited for a time in practice as their exercise may depend on financial, educational or temporal resources. Neither are citizenship rights and obligations independent of one another. The fulfilment of obligations, for example civil and political obligations, is dependent on access to economic, social and cultural rights and the enhancement of rights on a broad basis is dependent on widely based participation or at least representation in decision-making processes.

The papal encyclical *Pacem in Terris* deals with the linkage of rights and obligations in a very interesting way. It links a person's right to a decent standard of living with the duty of living that life appropriately; it links the right to investigate the truth freely with the duty of pursuing the truth ever more completely and profoundly. It points out that in human society, one person's natural right means there is a duty for other persons: the duty of acknowledging and respecting the right in question. It goes on to state that:

> Those who claim their own rights, yet altogether forget or neglect to carry out their respective duties, are people who build with one hand and destroy with the other ... A well ordered human society requires that men and women recognise and observe their mutual rights and duties ... It is not enough to acknowledge and respect every person's right to the means of subsistence. One must also strive to ensure that she/he actually has enough in the way of food and nourishment.

What Are Social, Economic and Cultural Rights?

If Ireland is to develop in a way that ensures everyone has 'the economic, social and culture rights indispensable for his/her dignity and the free development of his/her personality', as the UDHR requires, then these rights should include:

• The right to sufficient income to live life with dignity.
• The right to work.

- The right to appropriate accommodation.
- The right to essential healthcare.
- The right to relevant education.
- The right to participate in the cultural life and heritage of their community and wider society. This includes the right of minorities to have their cultures respected.
- The right to participate in shaping the decisions that affect their lives.

Everyone in Ireland should see these rights vindicated as a matter of course. Adequate resources exist in Ireland and in the European Union to deliver on each of these rights at this time. Failure to recognise them and to ensure that they are accessed by all should be recognised for what it is – a failure of political will to treat all people in this country or in the EU fairly and justly.

The Question of Justiciability

Whether these socio-economic and cultural rights should be justiciable or not (in the sense of being amenable to judicial or quasi-judicial vindication) is a contentious issue. Many argue that these rights should be defined as standards rather than as justiciable rights. I believe it is crucial that policy-making is linked to a set of clear standards and that outcomes should be measured against agreed benchmarks. They should also recognise the rights of individuals and groups to participate in processes relevant to the realisation of their rights.

Whether or not this is sufficient remains a debatable point. In an ideal world, these rights would be justiciable. However, they will not be recognised as such until the political process is prepared to acknowledge their importance in the expanding and evolving understanding of human rights. Therein lies one of the major challenges facing the political process at this time.

To ensure that the recognition of social, economic and cultural rights goes beyond words, however, it is essential to address the question: how can such rights be made justiciable? In particular, how can this be done in a way that respects the political process and does not destroy the balance of power between the judicial and the political dimensions of society, while also respecting the social, economic and cultural rights of people?

I suggest the following as a viable way forward that would respect concerns expressed particularly by politicians, while also respecting the need for people's rights to be justiciable. My proposal has a number of components.

First, these social, economic and cultural rights should be recognised explicitly in the Irish Constitution of 1937. Following this recognition, there would be a requirement to pass legislation ensuring that these rights could be vindicated. This could be achieved without producing a non-viable situation that would see every individual pursuing, for example, access to appropriate accommodation, all the way up to the Supreme Court.

Second, there would be a legal requirement on each incoming government to set out concrete targets on each of the range of social, economic and cultural rights recognised in the Constitution. The specific list of rights would already be set out in legislation and should cover the list outlined above or some similar range of rights.

Finally, the targets set out in such legislation would have to be for specific periods of time, e.g. two and four years (these particular time frames would also be set out in the legislation). Failure to achieve these targets would give rise to justiciable issues that could be assessed on a class action or similar basis but not on the basis of every individual bringing their particular case to court.

I believe a mechanism along these lines should be developed and put in place in all EU states. It would mean that social, economic and cultural rights were placed on the same level as civil and political rights. It would also mean that the EU's over-concentration on the economic dimension would be rebalanced at least in part by a growing recognition of the importance of the social dimension to citizens in all EU member states. Nothing could be truer to the spirit of Article 22 of the UDHR.

(1) EVERYONE HAS THE RIGHT TO WORK, TO FREE CHOICE OF EMPLOYMENT, TO JUST AND FAVOURABLE CONDITIONS OF WORK AND TO PROTECTION AGAINST UNEMPLOYMENT.

(2) EVERYONE, WITHOUT ANY DISCRIMINATION, HAS THE RIGHT TO EQUAL PAY FOR EQUAL WORK.

(3) EVERYONE WHO WORKS HAS THE RIGHT TO JUST AND FAVOURABLE REMUNERATION ENSURING FOR HIMSELF AND HIS FAMILY AN EXISTENCE WORTHY OF HUMAN DIGNITY, AND SUPPLEMENTED, IF NECESSARY, BY OTHER MEANS OF SOCIAL PROTECTION.

(4) EVERYONE HAS THE RIGHT TO FORM AND TO JOIN TRADE UNIONS FOR THE PROTECTION OF HIS INTERESTS.

ARTICLE 23

Jack O'Connor

President of SIPTU

The Universal Declaration of Human Rights was adopted and proclaimed by the General Assembly of the United Nations in December 1948. Like many great historic documents, it reflected fundamental human aspirations but did so within a specific historical context. The year 1948 was a turbulent time. It witnessed the Berlin blockade which led to the onset of the Cold War in earnest, the assassination of Mahatma Ghandi and the partition of the Indian subcontinent, the first Arab–Israeli war, the Communist victory in the decades-long Chinese civil war and the outbreak of wars of liberation across a swathe of south-east Asia.

In Europe, we saw the first tentative steps towards greater co-operation between states. The Brussels Treaty pledged Britain, France, Belgium, Luxembourg and the Netherlands to a fifty-year alliance aimed at social and economic progress, as well as opposition to war as a means of resolving differences. All of these states called for the rehabilitation of Germany within the family of European nations and the Movement for European Unity was launched in The Hague.

It was a time of great material hardship caused by the devastation of war, but it was also a time of great hope for ordinary working people and their representative organisations. There was widespread recognition of the tremendous role that the labour movement had played in the struggle against fascism and the defeat of Hitler. This is implicit in many articles of the UDHR, but none more so than Article 23, which guarantees everyone 'the right to work' and 'to just and favourable conditions of work', as well as 'protection against unemployment'.

Thirty years before we managed to pass our first employment equality legislation, the UDHR proclaimed 'the right to equal pay for equal work' and the right of all 'to just and favourable remuneration ensuring for himself [sic] and his family an existence worthy of human dignity'. Since 1948, we have made some stuttering progress towards implementing the latter right, but even during our recent and unprecedented boom, 18 per cent of the population remained at risk of living in poverty, 2 per cent above the EU average, and 7 per cent of people actually lived in poverty. The figure was much higher for those who were unemployed and, as we all know, unemployment is currently rising at an accelerating rate (CSO, *Measuring Ireland's Progress 2007*).

Unfortunately, when it comes to the fourth and most fundamental right asserted in Article 23 – that 'everyone has the right to form and to join trade unions for the protection of his [sic] interests' – we have actually retreated in recent years. Individualised rights have been used quite skilfully by the neo-liberals in both political and business manifestations to undermine collective rights, such as the right to collective bargaining.

This is not just an Irish phenomenon – we have seen it right across Europe and it is a process, I regret to say, which has been aided and abetted by the courts. Recent judgments of our own Supreme Court and of the European Court of Justice have effectively put the freedom to provide goods and services under EU law ahead of the freedom to protect the workers who supply those goods and services.

All of this has been done in the name of the consumer, conveniently forgetting that the vast majority of consumers must also work for a living in order to avail of all these goods and services. In Ireland, the impact of this hijacking by the individual rights agenda has been even greater than elsewhere in Europe because we are virtually alone in having no right to collective bargaining enshrined in domestic law.

The consequences can be seen everywhere and are borne most heavily by the most vulnerable producers of goods and services – migrant workers. Many of them are casualised agency workers often physically and socially isolated from the wider community. They include people such as Latvian women picking mushrooms for less than €3 an hour or Serbian electricians on €4 an hour.

This phenomenon can affect whole sectors. Take, for example, provincial hotels, where 37 per cent of the workforce is made up of migrants – and the figure is over 60 per cent in some parts of the country – and where only 8 per cent of such workers are in a union.

This sector used to be highly unionised, and one legacy of that era is the existence of an Employment Rights Order (ERO) that lays down minimum conditions for many hotel workers. While the wage rates in that sector are not much above the national minimum wage, the ERO provides other important entitlements, such as occupational pensions, sick leave and holidays.

A similar threat has been posed to the Registered Employment Agreement (REA) in the highly unionised, and much better paid, electrical contracting industry. REAs provide similar protection concerning pay and conditions to EROs and are negotiated between unions and employers before being registered with the Labour Court. REAs have existed for seventy years and have served both sides of industry well.

Between them, these two mechanisms have provided basic protections for hundreds of thousands of workers in this country. Without a legal right of collective bargaining to fall back on, many workers will face even greater levels of exploitation in the future, especially from companies that refuse to recognise unions and seek to use the courts as a weapon to deny people rights enshrined in the spirit and letter of the UDHR.

Ironically, one of the great truths the UDHR is founded on is that rights enshrined in law are necessary to protect the weak against the strong. Regrettably, the law is a lot more accessible to the rich than the poor. For almost 200 years, successive governments of all political persuasions in Britain and Ireland have recognised this and accepted that collective bargaining is a far more desirable way of resolving disputes between employers and employees than the prohibitively expensive and highly combative alternative of contract law.

Contract law is based on the notion that both parties are roughly equal in resources as well as rights. This has always been patently untrue when an individual worker has been in dispute with his employer. Today, the unions that represent workers are themselves constantly depicted as vested interest groups on a par with business enterprises. In fact, union leaders are often referred to as union 'bosses', a term rarely used any more in relation to real bosses, who tend to be described with less pejorative terminology, such as 'chief executives', 'directors' or 'business leaders'.

But it is no more realistic to equate even a large trade union and its economic resources with the business organisations it must contend with. The legal colonisation of industrial relations under the guise of championing individual rights is one of the great injustices of our time. Workers do not want the 'right' to hire a lawyer at ruinously expensive rates to fight their corner for them. They want the right to fight their own corner and to do so through their own organisations, led by people they elect and who are answerable to them.

To achieve this basic freedom, which is so central to the lives of over 75 per cent of our workforce, we need Article 23.4 of the UDHR, which recognises the right to collective bargaining, enacted into law by the Irish government – and we need it now!

The world that gave birth to the Universal Declaration had learned through over thirty years of war and revolution that a historic compromise was needed between capital and labour to make the planet a safe place for human beings to live and pursue their dreams. As that collective memory recedes, corporate greed, marching under the banner of consumer-based and individualised rights, is trying to turn the clock back. The champions of such an approach must not succeed or we will have to learn the lessons of history all over again.

EVERYONE HAS THE RIGHT TO REST AND LEISURE, INCLUDING REASONABLE LIMITATION OF WORKING HOURS AND PERIODIC HOLIDAYS WITH PAY.

ARTICLE 24

Seán Óg Ó hAilpín

Cork hurler

For me, Article 24 of the Universal Declaration of Human Rights means that I have the right to pick up a hurley. In Article 24, I see the right to stand in a field, frozen, in lashing rain with a bunch of other lads. I see the right to sport and am reminded again of the importance it has played in my life.

As a young boy, I grew up in Australia with my Fijian mother, Emilie, and my father, Seán, a native of County Fermanagh. At the age of eleven, we left our home to move right across the world to the land of my father. To be honest, before then, I was never quite sure if Ireland even really existed.

My dad had given me a hurley when I was younger and, every September, we were woken in the middle of the night to gather around the radio to listen to reports of a game called hurling in a place called Croke Park, but it didn't feel real to me.

When I arrived into Cork city in 1988, I realised that my life had changed suddenly, and completely. I remember my first day in school. There I stood in front of my new classmates, a half-Fijian, half-Irish boy, straight from Australia. My new teacher introduced me to my classmates: 'We have a new boy, his name is Seán Óg and he comes from Australia.' One of my new classmates turned to our class map of Europe and pointed at Austria. 'Is that it, sir? Is that where he is from?' I knew then that I was far from my old home.

But I was to find a new home in 'the Mon', North Monastery CBS, where I was introduced to hurling properly. We were probably, though I'm not sure, the first Fijian-Irish family to arrive in Cork's northside, but I am very sure that we were the first Fijian-Irish boys to stand on the hurling pitch.

It didn't matter to the lads I played with in the Mon, or went on to play with for my club, Na Piarsaigh, that my brothers and I were born in Fiji or Australia. It wasn't about the colour of our skin, it was about the game. Regardless of my colour or that I was from a different place, I was free to step onto the pitch and pick up a hurl and sliotar like anyone else. Nobody cared where I was from. They didn't care what I looked like or how I sounded. It was about the team. It was about lifting the sliotar, passing it on, playing with the team.

That's sport. It's a universal language. It's something that you can play with complete strangers who don't speak your language or know your culture or it's something you can spend a lifetime trying to perfect with your closest friends.

When I first arrived in Ireland, I was an outsider and a stranger. But, through playing hurling, I became as much a part of the community as a boy or girl born and raised on the northside. The freedom that afforded me, the idea that a foreigner can come into a community and play a sport that is the essence of this country, had a huge impact on the way my life turned out.

After a while, I wasn't 'Seán Óg the Fijian'. I was known by my name, Seán Óg.

I was fortunate enough to go on to have the opportunity to represent my county, to wear the same colours as Christy Ring, to stand on the steps of the Hogan Stand and to hold the Liam McCarthy Cup aloft in front of tens of thousands of my countymen and women and thank them in our own language. And I got to bring the trophy home to the Mon, for the next generation. The self-belief that playing GAA instilled in me has brought me to a very privileged place.

My story demonstrates the opportunity sport, or any form of leisure activity, can afford people to integrate into a community. For me, it was the GAA and hurling. For other children in Ireland today, it could be soccer or rugby or swimming or tennis.

It's easy for people who are not into sports to miss out on how important a role it has to play. Participation in sport and leisure activities can help break down artificial barriers of race and class. For me, it opened doors to my community. It integrated me in a new culture. I see in Article 24 the right to participate like anyone else in rest and leisure activities, the exact same opportunity that I took when I arrived in Cork.

Last November, I read in the newspaper about a talented sixteen-year-old hurler playing at corner-forward with Lucan Sarsfields. Sujon Alamgir is from Bangladesh. The article ended with him saying, 'I've played at Croke Park before for my school and I'd love to play there for Dublin at senior level.'

I can't wait for that to happen. I can't wait to see players from Nigeria or Russia, Poland or the Philippines turning out at Croke Park in their county colours. And you can be sure it's going to happen. One in ten people living here today was born outside Ireland. Increasingly, sporting organisations like the GAA, the FAI, the IRFU and others are working to ensure that integration and anti-racism are not just set out in worthy policy documents, but that they are a reality at national and local level and that they exist on playing fields and in sports centres.

Sadly, the role of sporting organisations in doing this looks like it will become more and more important. In 2007, the gardaí received 180 reports of racism, up from a figure of 66 incidents in 2004. These included damage to property, assaults, harassment and incitement to hatred. Yet funding for the Office of the Minister for Integration was cut by 26 per cent in the 2008 budget and the National Consultative Committee on Racism and Interculturalism (NCCRI) has been abolished.

For decades, the GAA played a role in supporting and developing communities in rural and deprived parts of the country where the state had failed. Now, with the GAA, the people working hardest in your community to ensure our new communities are not left behind or isolated could be your local soccer coach or the people running swimming lessons. Through that kind of participation, I believe the real promise of Article 24 in Ireland will be realised by ensuring that we all have access to rest and leisure activities with people new to our country.

(1) EVERYONE HAS THE RIGHT TO A STANDARD OF LIVING ADEQUATE FOR THE HEALTH AND WELL-BEING OF HIMSELF AND HIS FAMILY, INCLUDING FOOD, CLOTHING, HOUSING AND MEDICAL CARE AND NECESSARY SOCIAL SERVICES, AND THE RIGHT TO SECURITY IN THE EVENT OF UNEMPLOYMENT, SICKNESS, DISABILITY, WIDOWHOOD, OLD AGE OR LACK OF LIVELIHOOD IN CIRCUMSTANCES BEYOND HIS CONTROL.

(2) MOTHERHOOD AND CHILDHOOD ARE ENTITLED TO SPECIAL CARE AND ASSISTANCE. ALL CHILDREN, WHETHER BORN IN OR OUT OF WEDLOCK, SHALL ENJOY THE SAME SOCIAL PROTECTION.

ARTICLE 25

John Monaghan

National Vice-President of the Society of St Vincent de Paul

Ireland 2009 Does Not 'Do Poverty'

Article 25 of the Universal Declaration of Human Rights could easily have been written by Frederic Ozanam and his colleagues when they founded the Society of St Vincent de Paul (SVP) in Paris in 1833. Frederic Ozanam consistently stressed the innate dignity of the human person and the duty of care and responsibility each one of us shares for our neighbours irrespective of race, creed, country of origin or personal and financial circumstances. Sadly, the daily experience of our more than 1 million members worldwide is that the underlying principles and aims of Article 25 have yet to be achieved in many countries, including Ireland.

The mission statement of the SVP here in Ireland contains three central pillars that encapsulate the essence of our work. These are:

1) To be available to offer friendship and support, financial and emotional, to all who seek our assistance.
2) To work with people in need to enable them to achieve financial and social independence so that they can live with dignity in control of their own lives.
3) To identify the structural causes of poverty and exclusion in Irish society and to work for their elimination.

The last pillar informs our advocacy work and draws inspiration from the words of Frederic Ozanam when he reminded members of the SVP that: 'You must not be content with simply tiding the poor over a poverty crisis; rather you must examine the root causes of poverty and injustice in society and work for their elimination.'

Unfortunately, those words are as relevant in 2009 as they were in the 1840s.

Over the past decade, Ireland experienced unprecedented economic growth, increased employment and improvements to the physical infrastructure of the country. At an individual level, many of us had more cash and access to cheap credit. We spent our money on new cars, more foreign holidays, buying overseas properties and watched our young people leaving Ireland to travel and work overseas out of desire rather than necessity. Indeed, one of the by-products of our economic success saw traditional emigration replaced by the significant inward migration of foreign workers and asylum-seekers, all seeking a better life in what was a new, vibrant Irish economy, hoping that in Ireland, the promises of Article 25 might be fulfilled.

However, while economically Ireland performed spectacularly, our performance in addressing deep-rooted social problems and addressing the noble principles of Article 25 has been a lot less impressive. Sadly, our increased affluence was accompanied by an increased level of materialism and individualism. We were told that instant personal gratification and satisfaction are not only possible but commendable, and consequently we saw the emergence of a 'because you're worth it' mentality.

It certainly has to be acknowledged that the lives of many of the people assisted by the SVP did improve over the past decade. This was achieved through a number of factors: increased employment, particularly part-time employment for women; the introduction of the minimum wage; and increases in welfare payments and pensions. It must also be acknowledged that developments such as the National Anti-Poverty Strategies, the social inclusion provisions of the National Development Plan and the increasing emphasis on social inclusion as part of the social partnership process have had a positive impact. So, in fairness, the state attempted to eliminate poverty and reduce social exclusion.

But given that the mission of the SVP is to offer friendship and support to help people achieve independence and to work for social justice, we have to ask the awkward question: did we as a country use our newfound wealth wisely and fairly? Did we manage to eliminate poverty, or even reduce it substantially? In particular, what about those who still need to seek the assistance of the SVP and other charities? Are they, as some suggest, just malingerers or welfare scroungers? In essence, after a period of dramatic economic growth, can we as a nation claim to be addressing the basic human rights set out in Article 25?

Unfortunately, despite evident progress and improvement in the lives of poorer people, the past decade can also be characterised by our failure as a society to share our newfound wealth more equitably. Consequently, the gap between those on the top and bottom incomes remains as far apart as ever. While there has been a significant reduction in consistent poverty, we still have over 7 per cent of the population (or over 280,000 people) living on a very low income and suffering deprivation of basic necessities, such as food, heat, clothing, etc.

Today, we still have over 19 per cent of the population (about 800,000 people) living 'at risk of poverty'. These people live every day on the edge of a financial and emotional cliff. They wake each morning worried that something unexpected might occur during the day to push them over the cliff.

Yet one of the greatest challenges the SVP faces is convincing the majority of people that there are still poor people who struggle each day to live in the Ireland of 2009. And even if it is accepted that poverty still exists, a common reaction is that the poor have only themselves to blame for this – 'sure, weren't there plenty of jobs'.

But if there is no poverty in Ireland, and all the principles of Article 25 are being met, can someone please explain why the SVP is now spending over €43 million each year on the apparently non-existent poor and their non-existent problems? Why, in what was one of the wealthiest countries in the world, did the SVP still have to spend more than €4.8 million on food, over €3.5 million on fuel and energy, €2.5 million tackling educational disadvantage and nearly €8 million on general bills? Why do our 9,500 members make over 350,000 visits and provide over 2 million free volunteer hours visiting and assisting the apparently non-existent poor here in Ireland?

The sad reality is that members of the SVP know not just what the problems are, but where they are and who it is that's struggling with those problems. And so the SVP will continue to ask those awkward questions, questions that tend to and should make politicians, government officials and the wider public a little uncomfortable, questions that are, in fact, prompted by Article 25.

Poverty Levels

- Why, after more than ten years of unprecedented economic growth, do we have nearly 7 per cent of the population (nearly 280,000 people, about 100,000 of whom are children) still living in consistent poverty and nearly 800,000 people living at risk of poverty?
- Why, if we care so much about family life, is it that those most at risk of poverty are households with children, and why is it that among that group single-parent households are the most vulnerable?

Health

- Why is it that, in 2008, just over 21 per cent of the population had a full medical card on income grounds compared with well over 30 per cent a decade ago?
- Why is it still the case in Ireland that the poorer people get sick more often, wait longer for services and, sadly, die younger than the rest of the community?

Housing

- Why, following the housing boom that resulted in the construction of 80,000 new housing units per year, do we still have nearly 44,000 households (about 140,000 people) on waiting lists for social housing?
- Why does the state continue to have to spend nearly €400 million per year in rent supplement payments to private landlords, often for very poor accommodation, for social welfare recipients on housing waiting lists?

Education

- Why do we still have one of the worst records of early school leaving in Europe?
- Why do we still not have a proper school meals programme and a school book scheme to ensure that children coming to school hungry are provided with a meal and have books to work with?
- Why do we still have large numbers of vulnerable adults and young people struggling with literacy and numeracy problems that severely hinder their ability to participate in society?

To paraphrase the well-known election slogan, it's a case of 'a lot done – but a hell of a lot more to do' before we can state that we are in full compliance with the principles set out in Article 25.

(1) EVERYONE HAS THE RIGHT TO EDUCATION. EDUCATION SHALL BE FREE, AT LEAST IN THE ELEMENTARY AND FUNDAMENTAL STAGES. ELEMENTARY EDUCATION SHALL BE COMPULSORY. TECHNICAL AND PROFESSIONAL EDUCATION SHALL BE MADE GENERALLY AVAILABLE AND HIGHER EDUCATION SHALL BE EQUALLY ACCESSIBLE TO ALL ON THE BASIS OF MERIT.

(2) EDUCATION SHALL BE DIRECTED TO THE FULL DEVELOPMENT OF THE HUMAN PERSONALITY AND TO THE STRENGTHENING OF RESPECT FOR HUMAN RIGHTS AND FUNDAMENTAL FREEDOMS. IT SHALL PROMOTE UNDERSTANDING, TOLERANCE AND FRIENDSHIP AMONG ALL NATIONS, RACIAL OR RELIGIOUS GROUPS, AND SHALL FURTHER THE ACTIVITIES OF THE UNITED NATIONS FOR THE MAINTENANCE OF PEACE.

(3) PARENTS HAVE A PRIOR RIGHT TO CHOOSE THE KIND OF EDUCATION THAT SHALL BE GIVEN TO THEIR CHILDREN.

ARTICLE 26

Declan Kelleher

President of the Irish National Teachers' Organisation (INTO)

The commitment in Article 26 of the UDHR to free elementary education is expressed in an Irish context through Article 42.4 of the Irish Constitution of 1937, which declares that:

> The state shall provide for free primary education and shall endeavour to supplement and give reasonable aid to private and corporate educational initiative and when the public good requires it, provide other educational facilities or institutions …

This constitutional support for free primary education is given specific expression in the *Rules for National Schools.*

Under the heading 'Key Issues in Primary Education' in the introduction to *Curaclam na Bunscoile*, the current Irish primary curriculum statement, we read that: 'Each child is entitled to the best quality of education and it is the responsibility of the state to provide for this through the education system.'

Therefore, in Ireland, the rhetorical commitment to free primary education as outlined in the Universal Declaration of Human Rights is in place. The question to be examined is whether or not the Irish state lives up to these commitments and aspirations.

The Irish primary curriculum comprises Gaeilge, English, Mathematics, Social, Environmental and Scientific Education (SESE), Social, Personal and Health Education (SPHE), Physical Education and Arts Education.

But is it possible for Irish primary schools to implement this curriculum in full, given the resources provided by the state? In my experience as a primary school principal for the past twenty-nine years, each one of which has been punctuated by significant and very necessary fundraising for my school, I would have to state clearly that primary schools are not adequately funded to fulfil their mandate in implementing the primary school curriculum. The result is that schools have to seek the necessary resources elsewhere and, in most cases, parents are forced to step in and make up the shortfalls in funding incurred by their local school. The implications of this are clear and mean that primary or 'elementary' education is clearly not free in Ireland. Undoubtedly, Ireland has progressed over the past forty years in terms of the resourcing levels that are available to primary schools, but unfortunately, there are still major deficits.

Three examples will suffice to highlight the extent and effect of the underfunding of schools by central government.

Full implementation of the English language curriculum requires that each school should have a dedicated school library as well as individual class libraries. This is explicitly outlined in the Curriculum Statement, which reads: 'The ready availability of a wide variety of suitable books is essential in all schools. Such a resource will cater for the needs of every area of the curriculum and should be provided through the establishment of a well-stocked school library in every school.'

However, insufficient resources dictate that many schools cannot stock a central library and, due to the overall shortage of built infrastructure, many other schools are unable to dedicate a spare room for permanent library usage.

In the area of Physical Education, schools struggle to implement many of the curriculum strands, such as aquatics and gymnastics. In order to implement the aquatics section, schools must hire out swimming pools, hire lifeguards and organise transport for pupils. As no central departmental resources are allocated to this area, parents and the local community must, inevitably, fund the deficit. The same applies to gymnastics, as most primary schools lack a PE hall, so school communities, where possible, must seek out suitable sports halls, thus placing further costs in the way of parents.

The Curriculum Statement also describes technological skills as being 'important for advancement in education, work and leisure and integrates information and communications technologies into the teaching and learning process and provides children with the opportunities to use modern technology to enhance their learning in all subjects'.

But who provides the necessary hardware and software to allow this to happen? Again, it is the local education community of parents because, apart from a very basic monetary grant to primary schools made under the IT2000 initiative, state funds have not been made available to purchase, maintain, upgrade and replace schools' technology and the professional development of teachers has been minimal. Outside the three examples above, the areas of Science and the Visual Arts also place significant funding demands on school budgets.

So what does the state actually fund? In the main, the level of annual state funding available to a typical 100-pupil primary school consists of a capitation grant of €178 per child, together with an ancillary services grant of €145 per pupil and a small minor works grant to fund urgent essential repairs. In effect, the capitation grant is meant to cover all the day-to-day expenditure needs of the school and the ancillary services grant is meant to facilitate the employment of a secretary and caretaker. A typical 100-pupil school will struggle on a budget of €17,800, as its basic heating, cleaning, electricity, telephone, stationery, waste and water charges and insurance will absorb most, and often all, of this grant. Vital expenditure on classroom and other essential school equipment will have to be made from the school's own resources.

The same school also has a budget of €14,500 to fund the employment of a part-time secretary and caretaker, thus allowing the school to pay €7,250 to each per annum. The funding shortfall becomes glaringly obvious as the sum is insufficient to allow for anything approaching an adequate number of hours per week for secretarial and caretaking services. As both of these services are vital to the running of the school, this becomes a further cost on parent communities.

All of the primary school management authorities are united in their view that primary schools are underfunded. In a survey published by the National Parents' Council Primary (NPC) in February 2008, 90 per cent of the parents surveyed stated that their Parent Associations fundraise to cover running costs of the school and 74 per cent stated that they were asked for a voluntary contribution every year. According to the NPC, the results show that while primary education is supposed to be free, parents have to contribute significant amounts to keep schools running and parents can feel pressurised to contribute money they cannot afford. For decades, the Irish National Teachers' Organisation has led a campaign to significantly increase primary education funding in Ireland and its annual pre-budget submissions to government have consistently highlighted the inadequacy of primary school funding.

The 2007 OECD report *Education at a Glance* showed that, on average, OECD countries spend 6.2 per cent of their GDP on education, whereas Ireland spends just 4.6 per cent. It also showed that Ireland spends much less on primary education than on other parts of the education system. In terms of the built infrastructure for primary schools, there are also major deficits on capital expenditure in school building requirements in terms of the provision of modern suitable buildings with appropriately sized classrooms and the necessary range of ancillary rooms for special education, school principals, secretarial offices, parent rooms and, of course, PE halls. In many cases when building projects are finally commenced, local communities find themselves constantly raising funds to supplement those provided by the state.

Undoubtedly, some improvements in primary education have taken place over the past five years with regard to the recognition of and provision for pupils with special education needs. The appointment of significant numbers of resource teachers means that pupils assessed with recognised special educational needs are now entitled to individualised teaching time. However, many parents have had to access educational psychologists on a private fee-paying basis as the National Educational Psychological Service (NEPS) is not available in all regions of the country and, even where it is available, may only (because of under-staffing) provide a limited service to schools. Furthermore, there are major deficits with regard to speech and language therapists that force many parents to seek private fee-paying access to these services. In fact, waiting times for access to state-funded services are so excessive that many children are effectively denied a service, with severe consequences for their educational attainment.

Equal access to education is a right for all, but because of insufficient state funding, children from lower socio-economic communities are discriminated against. The state does attempt to counter educational disadvantage through Delivering Equality of Opportunity in Schools (DEIS), which targets children in 600 of the 3,200 primary schools in Ireland and provides additional funding and other supports together with reduced class sizes in the 150 schools serving communities with the highest concentrations of disadvantage. It is, however, a limited initiative particularly because it fails to integrate fully with the activities of other government departments providing supports for disadvantaged communities. A significant example of this is the failure to integrate health, social welfare and education services for disadvantaged children and the continued under-resourcing of the Education Welfare Service.

For decades, successive Irish governments have been content to allow parent communities and religious management in schools to subsidise its own inadequate funding of primary education. With the significant decline of the latter, more is being demanded of the former and it is becoming ever more apparent that, in Ireland, primary education is anything but free. What is required is that the state, once and for all, faithfully reflects its solemn commitments under Article 26 of the UDHR and Article 42 of its own Constitution by accepting its responsibilities to fully fund primary education.

(1) EVERYONE HAS THE RIGHT FREELY TO PARTICIPATE IN THE CULTURAL LIFE OF THE COMMUNITY, TO ENJOY THE ARTS AND TO SHARE IN SCIENTIFIC ADVANCEMENT AND ITS BENEFITS.

(2) EVERYONE HAS THE RIGHT TO THE PROTECTION OF THE MORAL AND MATERIAL INTERESTS RESULTING FROM ANY SCIENTIFIC, LITERARY OR ARTISTIC PRODUCTION OF WHICH HE IS THE AUTHOR.

ARTICLE 27

Theo Dorgan

Poet and writer

Sometimes, the best way to examine a thing is to look at its shadow.

Imagine a world where a child is forbidden to dance or sing, where the purchase and sale and playing of musical instruments is forbidden, where the galleries and concert halls are dank and shuttered, the cinemas and theatres converted to warehouses, the bookshops and libraries cleared, their contents piled in the streets for burning. Imagine a world where music is banned from the airwaves, where iPods and CD players may not be sold or traded, where films may not be made, where the archives of song, picture and story have been put to the flame.

And take it further. Prison for poets and singers, the confiscation, with attendant penalties, of brushes and pigments, musical instruments, cameras and recording devices, an all-pervasive web monitor to check that you're only downloading approved content.

Imagine that world, and push it further still. All science conducted in closed laboratories, the scientists imprisoned for life, forbidden to communicate the nature of their work, much less its results, to anyone outside the place to which they are confined. And this work overseen by a Committee of Public Safety that decides what is to be published, what is to be manufactured and released, to whom, under what circumstances and to what purpose.

A world where to be curious is to risk prison, or worse. A world where talent, a creative instinct, is the mark on the forehead of a doomed soul.

It sounds like second-rate science fiction, an imperfectly imagined dystopia, but here and there, even as I write, one or other of these denials is being enforced in one or another of the societies that make up our common world.

Why do we need to state these things as rights, that 'everyone has the right freely to participate in the cultural life of the community, to enjoy the arts and to share in scientific advancement and its benefits'?

Because the making and enjoyment of art and science is a free and ungovernable activity, and thus a perpetual challenge, active or latent, to the will to power that animates all government, no matter how apparently benign.

Because unless we state a right, it cannot be claimed or demanded or, ultimately, enforced.

Because an unstated right can scarcely be defended.

Because an unstated right, untended, unminded, will wither on the vine.

Well, good, we have stated our rights; what then?

Do we not have a duty of care to our common rights, as we have a duty of care to each other?

In the representative democracies, to bring the matter a little closer to home, how do we oblige our governments to foster these rights?

Few Western governments are prepared to baldly place obstacles in the way of the composing and performing of music, the writing and publishing of poetry and novels, the mounting of exhibitions, the practice of free inquiry in the sciences. Most societies practise some kind of censorship, but for the most part in these democracies, censorship is only rarely draconian and ideological; it is more usually a vulnerable attempt to codify and give expression to a loosely understood and always shifting sense of social boundaries.

Many governments, on the other hand, seem quite prepared to inhibit the practice and enjoyment of the arts through a strategy of neglect. This is not necessarily, and not always, from malice, at least not from active malice. It's simply that, today, a great number of people are drawn to the exercise of government who have themselves little interest or education in the arts, and simply do not understand the human consequences of failing to provide for the arts. Furthermore, and worse, many governments do not show any sign of understanding that they are in power with a responsibility to provide for our life in the arts, just as they are in power to provide for those other social goods we value and cherish.

Two doors down from me, as I sit here writing this on a winter evening, a neighbour's child is practising the fiddle. The radio downstairs is playing a Jimmy MacCarthy song. There's an Eithne Jordan painting on the wall in front of me. If I look out the window, I can visualise again that time last summer when we counted 24 guitars on the green, as the local teenagers settled in for a night of catcalling, amorous byplay, singing and playing, and more or less amiable socialising. Over there on Howth Head, Máire Mhac an tSaoi maybe has her pen in her hand, and if I set myself to make a census inside the radius of an hour's walk I can count on finding three publishers, five published poets, two playwrights, a handful of serious novelists, maybe a score of painters — and God alone knows how many 'amateur' painters, singers and players of instruments, habitual theatregoers, members of choirs, makers and owners of paintings and sculpture, thousands of library users, concertgoers ... the reader will take my point. This is the Ireland we actually live in.

The practice and enjoyment of art is the absolute signature of what it is we do when we do what we can to feel human, alive and grateful for it. To make and enjoy art, to invest our sense of being human in the making and enjoyment of art, of whatever kind, is a profound universal human value.

I grant, naturally, that much of what I am describing will, in some way or another, take place without the permission or support of the government of the day. Art is protean, as much refusal as it is claim, and a great deal of it happens without anything to underpin it except the quiet determination of its practitioners to get on with what it is they do.

Why, then, do I say that government has a duty to provide for the arts? Because the compact between government and governed rests on a single unassailable assumption, that we are governed, by consent, only to the extent that government is the active expression of who we are and what we value. The right to practise government confers no licence to deny the innate humanity of the governed, or any portion of that humanity; on the contrary, it confers a duty to actively seek out and provide for the expressed and implicit interests of the governed. Insofar as we value the practice and enjoyment of the arts as much as we do, government, if it is to retain its claim to act on our behalf, has a duty to provide for the expression of that value every bit as much as it is required to provide for our material safety and well-being, our health and our education, from that substance which we agree to surrender to government to spend on our behalf. Naturally, at a given moment, it is part of the burden of government to decide where immediate priorities lie, and to provide according to that judgement, and one accepts that the choices to be made are often difficult choices. Equally, however, the government is obliged to consider the welfare of the citizen in all its aspects, to take always the holistic view. In this regard, a certain responsibility falls on us, as citizens, to speak up for ourselves.

We may ask, then, to what extent the Irish government acts to safeguard our cultural rights, as citizens, under the terms of Article 27 of the UDHR. I have just finished a five-year term of service on The Arts Council/An Chomhairle Ealaíon, the statutory body for the promotion and support of art and artists in Ireland. This is a highly professional and well-managed agency, forward-looking, responsive and sensitive to needs and opportunities. As the primary (but not the only) conduit for financial support to the arts from the state, it has been inching slowly towards what might be considered an adequate level of funding. Legitimate demand for grant assistance (or investment, as I prefer to term it), from well-run service providers as well as from an increasingly numerous body of artists in all disciplines, runs to about €110 million at present. The audience for all this work is more or less the entire population of the state. In 2009, the council will have approximately €76 million to disburse, a drop of 10 per cent over the 2008 level. Does this signal a retreat from responsibility on the part of the government? If you view the business of the state as simply the management of the economy, it can be presented as fiscal prudence – code for 'only the bookkeeping matters'. If you view the state as an entity called into being in order to provide also for our deepest humanity, then the answer must be yes, it is a flight from responsibility, and flight of a shameful kind.

More shameful yet is the retreat from providing for the arts education of our children. In 2007, the Arts Council/An Chomhairle Ealaíon, working with the Department of Education and Science, produced *Points of Alignment: The Report of the Special Committee on Arts and Education*. The key recommendations of the report were framed to express the belief that the arts, their practice and enjoyment are part of the foundation of every human being, and must be provided for at every level of the education system if that system is to produce full, responsible citizens. For reasons that have yet to be explained, the then minister, her successor and the government have refused to sign up to even the basic recommendations of the report. What does that tell us? And what must we do about it?

EVERYONE IS ENTITLED TO A SOCIAL AND INTERNATIONAL ORDER IN WHICH THE RIGHTS AND FREEDOMS SET FORTH IN THIS DECLARATION CAN BE FULLY REALISED.

ARTICLE 28

Emily Logan

Ombudsman for Children

Article 28 has been described as the Universal Declaration's ultimate aspiration, that all rights should be enjoyed equally. Relatively late in the drafting process, it became apparent that, in the absence of legally binding obligations, the declaration was at risk of becoming a mere list of rights without any guidance on implementation.

Article 28 emphasises the political, legal and economic relations within states (social order) and between states (international order) to achieve its ultimate aspiration – the realisation of human rights.

In exploring how Article 28 has been relevant to Ireland, I am going to focus on aspects of the international order that flowed most directly from the Universal Declaration of Human Rights: the elaboration of universal human rights standards and the acceptance by states of the principle of international monitoring.

One of the primary motivations behind the elaboration of international human rights norms is to find agreement on what needs to be done. There are, of course, many other rich sources of guidance on what the entitlements of individuals and communities are, but it is precisely this variety which makes internationally agreed standards so important. Negotiations of diverse peoples with unique legal, philosophical and religious traditions are, indeed, complex. It is very difficult to develop a common ground between states with very different opinions. Such negotiations are, of course, subject to the vicissitudes of international politics and result in what are necessarily compromised texts based on drafts that might have been stronger. However, there is great value in the fact that they are internationally agreed by sovereign states, because such political endorsement can increase compliance with human rights standards. Without wishing to exaggerate the impact, the elaboration of human rights norms that are widely accepted by the international community play no small part in encouraging a state to progress its human rights agenda and, as a result, contribute significantly to shaping the international order.

The UN Convention on the Rights of the Child (UNCRC) is a good example to illustrate these points. It represents a significant milestone in the human rights approach to children and underpins all the work my office undertakes. Notwithstanding great differences of opinion between states on questions such as the definition of the minimum age of a child, freedom of religion and adoption, the convention was adopted by the UN General Assembly on 20 November 1989. The convention is more widely ratified than any other human rights treaty. Uniquely, it encompasses civil and political rights as well as economic, social and cultural rights in a single human rights instrument.

Read in conjunction with the jurisprudence and guidelines of the UN Committee on the Rights of the Child, the UNCRC gives a strong indication of how the rights of children in Ireland should be promoted and protected. When the state falls short of reaching those standards, it is easier to make an argument outlining the need to do better when those standards have been overwhelmingly endorsed by the international community and Ireland has committed itself to meeting them.

This brings me to the question of monitoring and of how the international and social orders interface at the national level. To put international human rights monitoring in context, it must be borne in mind that the concept of the international community having a legitimate interest in how another state treats its people is relatively new. Indeed, the inclusion of Article 28 in the UDHR sprang from the reticence on the part of states to enter legally binding agreements, not to mention subject themselves to international scrutiny. A range of mechanisms have developed since 1948 under the auspices of the United Nations and regional human rights bodies such as the Council of Europe and the African Union. These mechanisms have embedded the idea that states can be held accountable for the extent to which they are fulfilling their human rights obligations. Of course, the existence of such mechanisms does not guarantee their effectiveness, but the fundamental shift in the notion of state sovereignty and the role of international law vis-à-vis individuals within states is very significant.

I believe strongly that the presence of an international order in which international human rights standards are agreed by states and monitored by various mechanisms has had a very positive influence on the promotion and protection of human rights in Ireland. I would like to mention two examples to illustrate this point.

The first relates to the examination of Ireland's initial report under the UNCRC by the UN Committee on the Rights of the Child in 1998. The committee raised a number of concerns with the Irish government, including the absence of a national policy on children incorporating the principles of the convention; the lack of co-ordination among government bodies working on children's issues; and the lack of an independent national monitoring mechanism accessible to children and young people which could deal with complaints regarding violations of their rights. When the state was being examined by the UN Committee in 2006, it was in a position to report that a National Children's Strategy, underpinned by the principles of the UNCRC, had been put in place; that the Office of the Minister for Children had been established to address the lack of co-ordination on children's issues between government departments; and that the Office of the Ombudsman for Children had been established as an independent body to promote the rights and welfare of children in Ireland and handle complaints about public bodies, schools and hospitals.

The state has acknowledged that the momentum behind the changes came in no small part from the UN Committee's comments. The UN Committee on the Rights of the Child was not the first body to make those recommendations to the Irish government. For many years, Ireland's vibrant non-governmental sector campaigned for significant public policy changes for children. Indeed, as with the other UN treaty monitoring bodies, the Committee on the Rights of the Child often raises concerns that are first brought to its attention by non-governmental organisations and national human rights institutions. But there is a difference from the state's point of view in criticism emanating from domestic sources and criticism emanating from an international committee of experts, which can express an authoritative view on the extent to which the state is fulfilling the obligations to which it bound itself voluntarily.

The second example relates to the impact of a decision of the European Court of Human Rights on discrimination against non-marital children. For a long time, a child born to unmarried parents had very limited rights and was regarded in Irish law as *filius nullius*, or 'nobody's child'. In the *Johnston* case (1986), Ireland was found to have violated Article 8 of the European Convention on Human Rights by failing to provide for a regime in which a daughter born to parents who were not married to each other could enjoy a normal family life and have proper legal links with both her parents. In addition to pressure from groups acting for unmarried parents and their children, the *Johnston* case resulted in the enactment of the Status of Children Act 1987. The enactment of this legislation was not a panacea for the differential treatment of children based on the martial status of their parents, but it was a significant step forward in dealing with the stigma and negative effects of 'illegitimacy'.

The examples above are brief illustrations of the positive effect that international human rights mechanisms can have on law, policy and practice in Ireland. In my view, more has been achieved by the existence of international standards and monitoring mechanisms than could have been achieved by domestic pressure alone. International human rights standards provide objective benchmarks around which criticism of the state can be framed. This empowers domestic actors in the non-governmental and statutory sectors to hold the state to account for failing to fulfil its international obligations. The evolution of international monitoring mechanisms has further enhanced this process by enabling international judicial and quasi-judicial bodies to undertake their own analyses, often supported by domestic actors. Given the right conditions, this accumulation of constructively articulated criticism can and has led to significant change.

The processes I have sketched above are but a part of the just social and international order envisioned in Article 28 of the UDHR, but it is an important part. It is also one that continues to evolve. Over the past sixty years, great strides have been made in establishing benchmarks and mechanisms for holding states to account. However, we must never underestimate the power of individual and collective efforts external to the political system that have advanced Ireland's human rights agenda.

I hope that when we celebrate future anniversaries of the Universal Declaration of Human Rights, structures will be stronger still and have a greater capacity to achieve the declaration's ultimate aspiration of the realisation of human rights for all.

(1) EVERYONE HAS DUTIES TO THE COMMUNITY IN WHICH ALONE THE FREE AND FULL DEVELOPMENT OF HIS PERSONALITY IS POSSIBLE.

(2) IN THE EXERCISE OF HIS RIGHTS AND FREEDOMS, EVERYONE SHALL BE SUBJECT ONLY TO SUCH LIMITATIONS AS ARE DETERMINED BY LAW SOLELY FOR THE PURPOSE OF SECURING DUE RECOGNITION AND RESPECT FOR THE RIGHTS AND FREEDOMS OF OTHERS AND OF MEETING THE JUST REQUIREMENTS OF MORALITY, PUBLIC ORDER AND THE GENERAL WELFARE IN A DEMOCRATIC SOCIETY.

(3) THESE RIGHTS AND FREEDOMS MAY IN NO CASE BE EXERCISED CONTRARY TO THE PURPOSES AND PRINCIPLES OF THE UNITED NATIONS.

ARTICLE 29

Justin Kilcullen

Director of Trócaire

Debates over the relationship between the individual and society, and the rights and duties of each, can be traced back to the earliest philosophical thinking in Ancient Greece and Rome. These debates have focused on the key question of what individuals can legitimately demand from society, and what society – including the said individuals – in return has an obligation to provide. Over the centuries, this debate has flourished and thrived, becoming an extremely important subject matter for many of the greatest philosophers, academics and, of course, the leaders of the major religions.

In particular, the Catholic Church itself has a strong doctrine of rights and duties. It was Pope Pius XI who developed the notion of duties in Catholic thinking through the concept of the common good. In *Quadragesimo Anno* (1931), he asserted that people must respect each other's rights, fulfil their duties to one another and contribute to the common welfare of the community. This appreciation of the significance of human rights and duties was also demonstrated in 1948 by Cardinal Angelo Roncalli (then the papal nuncio in Paris), who provided considerable assistance to the drafters and promoters of the Universal Declaration of Human Rights. Decades later, Pope John Paul II referred to the declaration as 'one of the highest expressions of the human conscience of our time'.

Pope John Paul II's assessment was forthright and precise – the Universal Declaration of Human Rights is truly a magnanimous document, setting out a vision which was, as Eleanor Roosevelt said, 'for all people and all nations'. This bold proclamation asserts the respect and dignity of each individual person, affirming the human rights they hold. Achieving this was quite a remarkable feat, one which, arguably, we would find extremely difficult to replicate today if we were challenged to do so. Central to the declaration is Article 29, which reminds us that rights do not exist in isolation, that the correlative of rights is duties, without which rights would be unenforceable. It goes on to specify that a person's rights can be limited by 'the rights and freedoms of others, and … the just requirements of morality'.

For Trócaire, human rights are essential to development. They give us the moral and legal basis for our work. The violation of civil and political rights, economic, social and cultural rights, as well as the denial of the right to development and the right to participate, are considered by Trócaire as root causes of poverty. These rights violations are compounded by inequality, injustice, lack of accountability and power imbalances.

Just as the concept of rights is fundamental to development, the concept of duties is fundamental to rights. Duties command a force that moves us from *should* to *must*. They carry a sense of commitment, prioritisation and action. Essentially, duties facilitate the implementation of rights. They progress the rights discussion from an abstract framing of claims to the practical allocation of responsibility for action. Often when we discuss human rights duties, we talk about the duty to respect, protect and fulfil. This is a useful way of thinking about our duties. By 'respect', we mean that we must refrain from violating other people's rights; by 'protect', we mean that we should actively protect people from others violating their rights; and by 'fulfil', we mean that we should take necessary action to ensure that all human rights are met.

It is no accident that following the adoption of the UDHR, much of human rights law has been articulated in the form of the various duties of the state. In our world of nation states, the state is the natural institution that should be accountable for respecting, protecting and fulfilling human rights. But the responsibility of human rights also extends well beyond the state. In its preamble, the UDHR asserts the declaration as 'a common standard of achievement for all peoples and all nations ... every individual and every organ of society'. This ascribes human rights duties to so many others – to regional and local government, to the business and community sectors, to voluntary groups and organisations and, perhaps most importantly, to each of us individually.

It is human rights, together with duties, which give us our sense of individuality and also our sense of humanity. Like rights, duties really are our power. In respecting rights and fulfilling our duties, we claim our space and our place in society. When we willingly, or inadvertently, forfeit our duties, we disengage; we leave ourselves exposed and we give others motive to disregard us. We should value, guard and fulfil our duties, and the responsibility and power that they award us, as much as we value our rights.

Human rights duties are extremely important and relevant to us in Ireland in 2008. They shape how we see ourselves as a nation, how we envisage our position in the wider world and how we link, engage and interact with those outside Ireland. This is especially important to people in developing countries.

There are many ways we can, and do, contribute to respecting and promoting human rights. Our commitment to reach the UN target for Official Development Assistance (ODA) of 0.7 per cent of gross national product (GNP) by 2012 is one very significant way. Now, more than ever, with the impact of rising food and fuel costs on those in the developing world, it is essential that we maintain this promise to the citizens of those countries, given their disproportionate exposure to these challenges. Another is our overseas development work generally, through Irish Aid (the Irish government's official development assistance programme), development organisations (such as the non-governmental organis-ations) and the long-standing work of the missionaries, all of which are strongly supported by the Irish public. A further example is through the education of future generations. It is extremely important that we teach our children about their rights and duties, leading by example and, formally, through human rights education and development education in the school curriculum. The benefits of establishing these issues and principles at such an early age are long recognised internationally.

In April 2008, in his address to the UN General Assembly, Pope Benedict XVI declared: 'In the name of liberty, there has to be a correlation between rights and responsibilities, on the basis of which every individual is called to shoulder responsibility for his or her choices, while taking into account relations with other people.' As individuals, and as a nation, we are in a privileged position in that we can choose to take this responsibility onto our shoulders, we can question and challenge the inequality we see around us in Ireland and abroad, and we can affirm our belief in the fundamental dignity and worth of each and every individual, and the rights and duties we all hold. We have come a long way towards doing this, but it requires further commitment and real moral courage to complete this journey. Will we stand up for human rights?

NOTHING IN THIS DECLARATION MAY BE INTERPRETED AS IMPLYING FOR ANY STATE, GROUP OR PERSON ANY RIGHT TO ENGAGE IN ANY ACTIVITY OR TO PERFORM ANY ACT AIMED AT THE DESTRUCTION OF ANY OF THE RIGHTS AND FREEDOMS SET FORTH HEREIN.

ARTICLE 30

Emily O'Reilly

Ombudsman and Information Commissioner

Article 30 of the Universal Declaration of Human Rights may best be described as the declaration's triple lock, a safety mechanism crafted with an eye for those who might cherry pick from the preceding twenty-nine rights in order to subvert the very spirit of the UDHR. No one should latch on to one right – such as Article 19's freedom of expression, for example – in order to trample on another right, such as, perhaps, Article 7's prohibition on incitement to discrimination.

Does this suggest, therefore, a hierarchy of rights and, if so, can that hierarchy be maintained in all circumstances and across all cultures? As Ireland moves towards a multicultural model of society, are our own assumptions of an implicit hierarchy being challenged? Is there even universal acceptance that the rights enshrined in the UDHR are, in fact, 'universal'?

Much of 'rights speak' is couched in the language of public interest, the balancing of rights to achieve the so-called 'public good'. As cultures begin to mix, a further question arises: which public? When confronted with an inflow of different ideas, philosophies, other cultural norms and religions, what was formerly 'obvious' begins to appear less so.

In some instances where rights collide, the hierarchy seems relatively straightforward. A piece of journalism that demonises a race, nationality or culture would appear to so pervert the notion of the free expression of opinion that only the obdurate, the ignorant or the inherently racist could claim that it does not. A quasi-religious practice, such as female circumcision, which in many cases inflicts grave injury, surely cannot come under the freedom of religion umbrella of Article 18 under any circumstance.

The less stark cases are the challenging ones. For this country, the recent influx of immigrants, some of them from Muslim countries, throws up new balancing challenges and calls for a fresh contemplation of our perceived hierarchy of rights.

In early 2008, a Somali Muslim man – based in an asylum centre in Tralee, County Kerry – was to be given an award for raising funds for Amnesty International. It was reported that he told the organisers in advance that, because of his religious beliefs, he would not shake hands with the woman due to present the prize.

Initially, he was told that this would be fine: religious belief in the ascendant. Five minutes before the prize-giving, reportedly, he was told that the award would be given to someone else: gender equality in the ascendant. Cue confusion and upset all round. It was clear that the cultural context determined the hierarchy of rights in that situation. This suggests in itself the absence of a universal acceptance of how rights should be balanced.

As in other countries, much of the debate around the co-existence of Muslims within a predominantly Christian/Western culture focuses on a single piece of female clothing, the hijab, the head covering worn by many Muslim women under the fundamental set of rules of the Qur'an, in fulfilment of a religious obligation perceived as a divine command.

The hijab emerges onto the Irish high street not that long after our own female religious head covering – the mantilla – has largely stopped being worn inside Catholic churches. Some Catholic nuns continue to wear a veil, perhaps a closer analogy with the hijab, as the mantilla was not worn in other public places.

The reason why wearing the hijab jars with current cultural norms in Ireland is because of the cultural changes that have taken place in Irish society in relation to women's roles in both the domestic and public spheres. The mantilla, over time, became a symbol of gender inequality within the Catholic Church and rightly or wrongly – and one cannot generalise about the lot of the Muslim woman – the hijab is seen by some in the same light.

One Dublin-based Muslim theologian, Ali Selim, has questioned the relatively recent Western concern about the wearing of the hijab. 'Why now?' he asked in a 2008 *Irish Times* article. Is it because former generations were 'less interested in women's rights, or because they were less aware of Islam's so-called unjust attitude towards women'?

There is little appetite for exploring the cultural significance of the hijab, its origins, its symbolism, its place in Islamic culture, or even the fact that some Muslim women see in it the same emancipatory tool as Western women saw in the mini-skirt of the 1960s.

One culture views the covering of the female body as a weapon against the objectification of women's bodies. Another culture sees the free display of flesh as a marker of equality and sexual emancipation.

Both groups, in effect, make the same argument. Hijab-wearing Muslim women believe that much of Western-style female dress dehumanises women. A similar argument is made against the hijab. Both arguments are not without merit, yet arguably, the critical test is not about the head dress per se, but what lies beyond in the form of the economic, political and social rights enjoyed by the hijab-wearers on the one side and those enjoyed by the mini-skirt and Uggs brigade on the other. But even if those rights differ, does that mean that the rights hierarchy should always and in every circumstance put the Western notion of gender equality over tolerance for sincerely held religious beliefs? Ali Selim comments that Islam stresses women's dignity, founded on their humanity; nor does Islam grant men superiority or impose inferiority on women on a gender basis. They share a mission in this life. They have similar roles; they are equal but they are not the same.

So, when the Department of Education is asked to adjudicate on the wearing of the hijab in our state schools and an official, perhaps as a guide, consults the UDHR and glances at Article 30 in particular, which human right will he or she urge the minister to give precedence to? Will freedom of religion and thought and expression trump the other freedoms? Will Article 2 triumph – that which rules against discrimination of any sort of the grounds of, among other things, sex? Will the department see the hijab as an unthreatening, legitimate expression of a deeply held religious belief, or as a symbol of something less benign? Admittedly, the debate is rarely couched in those terms; more prosaic considerations around dress code and discipline are said to be at issue, but one can hardly ignore the elephant in the room.

In making that call, the UDHR, in my humble view, gives little guidance, although Article 29 does allow for some rights restrictions done 'by law'. It implies that some rights in some circumstances trump other rights, but what are the tools we should use to determine these matters? If, as a society, we are minded to be inclusive and tolerant, what are the limits of that inclusiveness and that tolerance? In this society, the argument over the hijab is not entirely about its religious symbolism. If that was the case, the walls of many Irish Catholic schools would be denuded overnight. It is, rather, about a Western view of another culture which sees in the hijab a symbol of culturally unacceptable gender inequality.

If the hijab is banned, is this cultural oppression? If young Muslim girls are allowed to wear it, will that not sit uncomfortably with our relatively recently arrived at view of women as being equal to men? Yet even the expression of that notion of equality – with its sliderule connotations does not resonate with certain other cultures, cultures where the 'correct treatment' of women is not bound up with a mathematical imperative for equality, but rather with a balancing out of capacities, duties and responsibilities. Western culture may well believe that the net result of that rarely, if ever, favours women, but that is not the view of many people from those cultures. Do we dismiss that or respect it?

The dilemma arises in other areas of contemporary cultural controversy. In his commentary on the fraught debate within the Anglican Church on homosexuality during the 2008 Lambeth Conference, *Irish Times* journalist Patsy McGarry, noting how one person's human right emerges elsewhere on the planet as another person's taboo, mused: 'To what extent is the promotion of human rights a Western colonial exercise?' He added: 'To what extent are so-called "self-evident truths" arising from the Judaeo-Christian tradition … simply by-products of particularly successful culture rather than being "truths" that genuinely have the universal application claimed?'

Indeed, we don't even need to look to Islam, or to African Anglicanism, to be confronted with that level of uncomfortable questioning. As I was writing this piece, the most eye-catching culture clash on the planet was taking place in the United States as the battle there – arguably between Barack Obama and Sarah Palin rather than Obama and John McCain – pitted liberal against conservative on issues including abortion, homosexuality, religious teaching in schools and same-sex marriage – issues that do indeed put one person's human right against another's 'taboo'.

Whither Article 30 in all of that? A valuable admonition perhaps, but precious little guidance.

'TO DENY ANY PERSON THEIR HUMAN RIGHTS IS TO CHALLENGE THEIR VERY HUMANITY.'

Nelson Mandela

AFTERWORD

Dr Vinodh Jaichand

Deputy Director of the Irish Centre for Human Rights, NUI Galway

Anniversaries are opportunities to reflect on the achievements of the past and to speculate a little on the future. The genesis of the Universal Declaration of Human Rights (UDHR) might well have destined it as an outcome of its time and generation. Today, it has exceeded the narrow expectations set for it in an imperfect world. In a perfect one, its presence would have been superfluous. The many outstanding contributions in this book bear testimony to the various expressions of rights, the quality of human beings and the perceptions of human rights. My thoughts are directed at locating the modern context of the UDHR and interpreting it as a living document. This is achieved through a brief account of the role of historical events in shaping the UDHR, the question of sovereignty of states, global economies and universal human rights and, finally, the protection of all human rights for all persons.

Most states in 1948 were content to vote for the UDHR for various reasons, including the fact that no legal obligation, as from a treaty, resulted from its acceptance. When the stakes were so low, little could be lost by participating. Ironically, one of the states which had abstained from voting for the UDHR was apartheid South Africa, whose representative observed that voting for the UDHR would, in time, bind states in the same manner as if they had signed a treaty. That is a conclusion that many human rights lawyers share today, sixty years after the birth of the UDHR, when they state that these norms are part of customary international law or reflect the general principles of international law. While there are a number who violate human rights frequently, this conclusion should be understood in the context that most states observe most of these norms most of the time, as stated by the renowned human rights expert, Louis Henkin.

In 1948, most of the colonial powers were willing to accede to the UDHR as an aspirational document. They emphasised that character in their legal systems and underplayed its importance while they were concerned about the declaration's possible incendiary potential in the colonies which were agitating for freedom. They were also keen to underscore their support for the UDHR because a failure to do so would place them in dubious company. Some of these preoccupations were prominent when the European Convention for the Protection of Human Rights and

Fundamental Freedoms, also known as European Convention of Human Rights (ECHR), inspired by the UDHR, was drafted a year later. The Western European states did not support socialist or communist ideals, a matter of great contention in that day and age. As a result, the ECHR left out the protection of social, economic and cultural rights, as this would have sent the wrong message about allegiances.

Subsequently at the international level, the effects of the Cold War were also being felt when the treaty supporting the UDHR was split into two along ideological lines: the International Covenant on Civil and Political Rights (ICCPR) and the International Covenant on Economic, Social and Cultural Rights (ICESCR). As early as 1947, it was agreed to have one international treaty on human rights. Indeed, a single such covenant was drafted in 1951 that contained protection for all human rights. The Western liberal states argued that civil and political freedoms were the bedrock of human rights, while the socialist states said there could be no human rights without social and economic rights. As a result, the socialist countries – Byelorussia, Czechoslovakia, Poland, Ukraine, Yugoslavia and the Union of Soviet Socialist Republic – abstained from voting. Included in this group was Saudi Arabia and South Africa, as mentioned earlier.

The two international covenants that enforced human rights took nearly two decades to be adopted and came into effect nearly thirty years after the first decision to have a single treaty in 1947. The lack of speed on the development and implementation of these standards, arising directly out of the UDHR norms, highlighted the reluctance of states to be constrained by international human rights. In effect, such participation diluted the sovereign right of states to do what they wanted on their territory. Human rights became the thin edge of the wedge against sovereignty, as few countries could officially claim the right not to respect them. The subsequent development of human rights in each of the original eight abstaining countries in the past sixty years would make interesting reading, but is unfortunately beyond the scope of this afterword. Interestingly, some recent research indicates that many of the former Soviet Union states relied heavily on all the norms of the UDHR in the development of their new constitutional democracies. Notwithstanding these historical constraints, the UDHR is today seen as the primary document that encapsulates the basic rights of all human beings in the world.

The political ideologies of that time and age are not static as mere historical facts alone. It is remarkable that, even though the Cold War ended about twenty years ago, so many countries continue to cling to the outmoded notion, in spite of so many judicial writings and court decisions around the world, that only civil and political rights are human rights. In an age that has so readily accepted the virtues of instantaneous communication and globalisation, many states, including Ireland, are not convinced that social, economic and cultural rights are really rights that are justiciable in our courts. If economic globalisation resulted in the removal of national boundaries for economic purposes so that the markets can determine our collective economic wealth, then all barriers to sovereignty have long since disappeared. Why do states continue to raise sovereignty against human rights to justify their positions?

Coincidentally, this sixtieth anniversary of the UDHR occurred when one of the greatest challenges to economic globalisation was taking place, when so many states – like Ireland, the United Kingdom, France, Germany, Iceland and the United States of America – have taken rapid measures to give financial aid from the state coffers to banks and other financial institutions. When economic, social and cultural rights are claimed generally in these states, the lack of funds and the spectre of taxes are immediately raised, once the sovereignty threshold is cleared. Yet billions of euros were sourced by governments without any of these clarion calls. Instead, they were labelled as necessary for our well-being. The question of resources is always an important one, and that is why the bailouts of financial institutions are more startling. The hypocrisy surrounding the lack of human rights protection has now begun to wear thin, notwithstanding the lip service paid in Vienna in 1993 to all human rights being universal, inalienable and interdependent.

The largest unfulfilled promise contained in the UDHR is the protection of economic, social and cultural rights, sixty years after the painstaking process of enumeration of all human rights. There is little doubt that many states are caught in a time warp and need to upgrade their understanding of human rights law in conformity with all the norms contained in the UDHR which protect human rights for all. Those norms have to be interpreted in the light of modern developments. If the development of the role of the Directive Principles of Social/State Policy in the Irish and Indian constitutions (where the latter was inspired by the former) is observed, it is difficult for any citizen to comprehend the legal constraints imposed on socio-economic rights. As Gandhi was highly impressed by the forward-thinking ideas contained in Article 45 of the Irish Constitution of 1937, he adopted the same principles for his country. The Indian courts have been active with public interest litigation on economic, social and cultural rights, while the Irish find themselves marooned and will not always recognise the rights that are cognisable by courts.

If more than 2.6 billion people in the world live on less than $2 a day, the rights contained in the UDHR are not fulfilled. For them, human rights are truly meaningless. If the Western liberal states – where resources are not expected to be as large a constraint – do not recognise these rights as rights, what persuasion remains for the developing world to do so using their best efforts? An inability to provide an incentive for all states through practised behaviour is the largest cause of erosion in human rights today.

There is little doubt that the UDHR has succeeded as a common standard for all nations if it compels us all to see the larger picture. The protection of economic, social and cultural rights is a part of that picture. The adoption of the UDHR is regarded as a formal act which demonstrated an international commitment that ought to be fulfilled by a state. If the UDHR is seen as an agenda for the implementation of human rights, many items can be ticked off as completed in sixty years. But there is much more to be done if we wish to claim any success.

LIST OF CONTRIBUTORS

NOELINE BLACKWELL is a solicitor and the director general of FLAC, the Free Legal Advice Centres, an Irish human rights organisation dedicated to the realisation of equal access to justice for everyone. She has previously worked as a solicitor in private practice with a particular interest in family law and in human rights law in general, refugee and immigration law in particular. She sits on the Law Society's Human Rights Committee and its Family Law and Civil Legal Aid Committees. She was a contributor to *The Law Society of Ireland: Human Rights Law* (OUP, 2007) and lectures on the topic of refugee law. She is a former chairperson of the Irish section of Amnesty International and was also a member of its EU Association board. She is a trustee of Front Line, the Dublin-based international foundation for human rights defenders at risk. She sits on the board of the Immigrant Council of Ireland.

DR KATHLEEN CAVANAUGH is chair of the Executive Committee of Amnesty International Ireland and is a lecturer in International Law at the Faculty of Law, Irish Centre for Human Rights (ICHR), National University of Ireland, Galway. She has undertaken numerous missions on behalf of Amnesty International including to Northern Ireland, Israel/Palestine and, more recently, to Iraq (where she focused on the conduct of the occupying powers with relation to detention and security). She has also conducted training for governmental as well as non-governmental organisations throughout the Middle East (Egypt, Israel/Occupied Territories, Jordan, Lebanon, Morocco, Syria,

Sudan and Yemen), India and the Republic of Ireland. She holds a BA in Political Science from the University of Connecticut, USA, a LLM (Distinction) from the Queen's University, Belfast, Northern Ireland (1998), and a PhD in Comparative Politics from the London School of Economics and Political Science (1997).

DENISE CHARLTON became chief executive officer of the Immigrant Council of Ireland in 2003. The Immigrant Council of Ireland is an independent immigrant human rights organisation. It advocates for the rights of immigrants and their families and acts as a catalyst for public debate and policy change. Prior to 2003, Denise was CEO of Women's Aid, an organisation working on gender-based violence. In both roles, she has been involved in representation at local, national and international levels on social justice issues. Denise has been appointed to a number of governmental bodies, including the Task Force on Violence against Women, the Women's Health Council, the Advisory Research Committee of the Crime Council and the National Consultative Committee on Racism and Inter-Culturalism, and is presently the Irish expert to the European Women's Lobby on violence against women. In a voluntary capacity, Denise is the co-chair of the Marriage Equality, a new initiative working for civil marriage for gay and lesbian people. Denise's background is in communications and organisational development in the commercial, statutory and voluntary sector.

NIALL CROWLEY is the former chief executive officer of the Equality Authority, a post he held until 2009 since its establishment in 1999. Prior to this, he worked in the community and voluntary sector on a wide range of equality issues. He has been a member of the National Economic and Social Forum (NESF) and the National Economic and Social Council (NESC). Niall Crowley is author of *An Ambition for Equality*, published by Irish Academic Press (2005).

Born in Cork, living in Dublin, **THEO DORGAN** is a poet and prose writer as well as translator, editor and documentary scriptwriter. He is a member of Aosdána and was a member of the Arts Council/An Chomhairle Ealaíon from 2003 to 2008. He has worked extensively as a broadcaster, mainly for RTÉ, for whom he presented arts and literary programmes on both radio and television for many years. His most recent publications include *Songs of Earth and Light*, translations of the Slovenian poet Barbara Korun (Southword, 2005), *Sailing for Home*, a prose account of a transatlantic journey under sail (Penguin, 2005), *A Book of Uncommon Prayer*, a collection of prayers ranging widely across world religions (Penguin, 2007) and *What this Earth Cost Us*, a collection of his poetry (Dedalus Press, 2008). Dorgan is a lifelong supporter of Amnesty International and has been a member of the Urgent Action Network for many years.

LIEUTENANT GENERAL DERMOT EARLEY joined the Defence Forces as a cadet in 1965. He was commissioned into the Infantry Corps in 1967 and appointed a platoon commander in the Recruit Training Depot at the Curragh. He specialised in Physical Training and Education and was appointed as an instructor at the Army School of Physical Culture (ASPC) in 1969. Lieutenant General Earley was appointed school commandant of the ASPC. From 1983 to 1987, he was desk officer for overseas operations and later for current operations in the Chief of Staff's Branch at Defence Forces Headquarters. On his return from an overseas posting in 1991, he was appointed as an instructor at the Command and Staff School of the Military College, and during 1994–95, he helped establish the United Nations Training School Ireland (UNTSI) in the Military College. Lieutenant General Earley served with UNTSO in the Middle East from 1975 to 1977. From 1987 to 1991, he served as the deputy military advisor to the secretary general of the UN. Lieutenant General Earley commanded the 81st Infantry Battalion with

UNIFIL (Lebanon) in 1997. In 2007, the government appointed him chief of staff of the Defence Forces.

KATHLEEN FAHY has worked with Ruhama since 2004. She spent a number of years in Africa, teaching in Tanzania and Zimbabwe. She worked with an Irish development agency for twelve years, seven of which were spent in Somalia managing an emergency and rehabilitation programme. On returning to Ireland, she took up the position she now holds with Ruhama. The focus of Ruhama's work is the provision of support to women in prostitution and women trafficked into the sex trade in Ireland. Over the years, Ruhama has provided a range of supports to women abused in the sex trade and has worked to change the public attitudes and policies which enable the exploitation of women through prostitution and trafficking.

MICHAEL FARRELL is a solicitor working for the Free Legal Advice Centres in Dublin. He is a member of the Irish Human Rights Commission and the Human Rights Committee of the Law Society. He is a former co-chairperson of the Irish Council for Civil Liberties. He previously worked as a solicitor in private practice, where he acted in criminal cases and in a number of defamation actions for members of the Birmingham Six, the Guildford Four, Judith Ward and other victims of miscarriages of justice. He has taken cases to the European Court of Human Rights and the UN Human Rights Committee under the International Covenant on Civil and Political Rights, which developed out of the Universal Declaration of Human Rights. He is a former journalist and he was an activist in the Northern Ireland civil rights movement in the late 1960s.

RONNIE FAY has been involved throughout her working life in the promotion of Traveller and Roma rights within Ireland and internationally, in the EU and UN contexts. She was also a founding member of the National Traveller Women's

Forum and the Irish Traveller Movement. She is actively involved in the Community Worker's Co-op, has represented the Community Platform in the negotiation of national social partnership agreements and currently represents the Community and Voluntary Pillar within the Department of Health and Children.

FR SEÁN HEALY is the director of CORI Justice. For more than twenty-five years, he has been active on issues of socio-economic policy in Ireland. Before that he worked for more than ten years in Africa. He holds a PhD in Sociology. Seán has worked on many government taskforces dealing with social and economic policy issues ranging from taxation to the labour market, from sustainability to poverty, from income adequacy to rural development. He has been a member of the National Economic and Social Council (NESC) since 1997. He has been a leading member of the Community and Voluntary Pillar since it was included in the social partnership process in Ireland in 1996. He has chaired the South Western Regional Drugs Task Force since 2004 and was a member of the Housing Forum from 2004 to 2007. Together with CORI Justice's other director, Brigid Reynolds, Seán has written or edited twenty-one books on public policy as well as three books on spirituality for social engagement. Their work has also been published in a wide range of other books and journals. Their book *Social Policy in Ireland* (first published in 1998, 2nd edition in 2006) has become a standard textbook on social policy in Ireland.

LIAM HERRICK is the executive director of the Irish Penal Reform Trust (IPRT), Ireland's leading non-governmental organisation in the area of penal policy. IPRT campaigns for progressive and evidence-led reform of the Irish penal system and is guided by the principles of respect for human rights within the penal system with prison as a last resort. He also teaches a course in international human rights law at the School of Politics and International Relations in UCD, and has previously taught a course on Human Rights Perspectives on Social Work at Trinity College, Dublin. Before joining IPRT in 2007, Liam worked as senior legislation and policy review officer with the Irish Human Rights Commission and has also worked with the Irish Council for Civil Liberties, the Law Reform Commission and the Department of Foreign Affairs. He is also a board member of the Children's Rights Alliance.

DR VINODH JAICHAND is the Deputy Director of the Irish Centre for Human Rights and a lecturer in International Human Rights Law at National University of Ireland, Galway. He was formerly associate professor and Dean of the law school at University of Durban-Westville. He served as national executive director of Lawyers for Human Rights for more than five years in South Africa. He has published books on Restitution of Land Rights in South Africa, Anti–Discrimination for the Judiciary, co-authored a report for Amnesty International (Ireland) on State and Institutional Racism in Ireland and numerous articles. Apart from the English language, he is published in Chinese, German, Portuguese and Spanish in numerous journals around the world. He has presented papers in more than twenty countries. He is a member of the Editorial Review Board of Human Rights & Human Welfare, of the Advisory Board of the Sur-International Journal on Human Rights, of the International Advisory Board of Diakonia, Jerusalem and he was Chair of the Board of Integrating Ireland. He has also contributed extensively to the Amnesty International (Ireland) Human Rights Based Training Programme.

BOB JORDAN is the Director of Threshold. Its aim is to secure a right to housing, particularly for households experiencing poverty and exclusion. He previously worked for the Dublin Simon Community. He holds an MA in International Relations and has published extensively on social policy, housing and equality issues.

DECLAN KELLEHER, president of the Irish National Teachers' Organisation, is a native of County Clare. He qualified as a primary teacher in St Patrick's College of Education, Drumcondra in Dublin and later studied in UCD (BA) and Trinity College (H Dip Ed). While in St Patrick's College, he was elected president of the students' union and has been actively involved in the INTO ever since. Since 1979, he has been principal of Corofin NS in North Clare. He is a former Branch Cathaoirleach of both the North Dublin and Ennis INTO branches and was elected to represent Clare, Tipperary and Waterford on the INTO Education Committee, where he served for eleven years before being elected in 1996 to the INTO Executive to represent the 2,500 teachers in these counties. As an INTO Executive member, Declan has been closely involved in the union's campaigns to highlight substandard school buildings, to secure adequate resourcing for primary education, to provide for children with special education needs in mainstream primary schools and to reduce class sizes. He currently represents the INTO on the National Council for Curriculum and Assessment.

JUSTIN KILCULLEN was appointed the director of Trócaire in 1993. An architect by profession, he worked for many years in Africa and Asia. He hails from Dublin and graduated as an architect from University College Dublin in 1975. From 1976 until 1981, he worked in low-cost housing in Tanzania and on the design and construction of refugee camps for Cambodian and Vietnamese refugees. Justin Kilcullen joined Trócaire as a project officer for Africa in October 1981. He served as Trócaire representative in Laos from 1988 until 1992. He is a past president of CIDSE, an international alliance of sixteen Catholic development organisations in Europe and North America. He is currently the president of Concord, the confederation of European development NGOs, representing more than 1,600 such organisations across the European Union.

EMILY LOGAN is Ireland's first Ombudsman for Children. She was appointed to this position by Her Excellency, President Mary McAleese, following an interview process involving fifteen children and young people and three adults. Established in 2004, the Ombudsman for Children's Office is an independent, statutory organisation that accounts to the Oireachtas. The primary aim of the Ombudsman for Children is to safeguard and promote the rights and interests of children and young people up to the age of eighteen. The office is one of a growing number of international offices dedicated to the promotion and safeguarding of children's rights, with a total of thirty-four across Europe. She has recently been appointed chair of the European Network of Ombudsmen for Children. Before Emily became Ombudsman for Children, she worked for twenty-two years in child health, where she worked mainly with children with chronic illness. She spent ten years in the UK in Great Ormond St Hospital and Guy's Hospital. She returned to Ireland, where for six years preceding her appointment she held two senior positions in public administration: Director of Nursing at Our Lady's Hospital for Sick Children, Crumlin, and later Director of Nursing at Tallaght Hospital.

ROSALEEN McDONAGH is a Traveller woman with a disability who works in Pavee Point Traveller Centre. She works in the area of violence against women and also has a remit regarding Travellers' health. Her degree from Trinity College Dublin in Theology, Ethnic and Racial Studies was her area of interest for her Masters, which was also obtained from Trinity. She was a candidate in two Seanad elections. Rosaleen is a playwright and enjoys reading fiction and creative writing.

DEARBHAIL MCDONALD from Newry, County Down, is the legal editor of the *Irish Independent*. A former news correspondent with *The Sunday Times*, Dearbhail has won a series of awards for her journalism work, most recently the Justice Media Award 2007 presented by the Law Society of

Ireland. Dearbhail, who began her journalism career in New York, is also a former Young Irish Medical Journalist of the Year. She is a member of the Law Council of the National University of Ireland, Maynooth, and holds an LL.B (Law) from Trinity College, Dublin as well as a first class Masters degree in Journalism from Dublin City University. Dearbhail, who frequently participates in current affairs broadcasting in Ireland and Europe, is a board member of Media Forum, a non-profit organisation working to advance the cause of Media Literacy Education in Ireland and to promote active media citizenship. A national judge and official mentor for the European Young Journalist of the Year Award, spanning all twenty-seven member states of the European Union and all candidate and potential candidate countries, Dearbhail also co-founded the Roberta Gray Feature Award for aspiring feature writers. Dearbhail is currently working with Manresa, the Jesuit Spirituality Centre in Dublin, to develop a leadership programme for young and emerging leaders.

JOANNA MCMINN is the former director of the National Women's Council of Ireland and a member of the Women's Human Rights Alliance. Joanna has been a feminist activist in the women's voluntary and community sector since 1981. She was the founding development worker of the Women's Education Project and director of the Women's Resource and Development Agency in Belfast until 1994. From 1994 to 2000, Joanna worked as an independent consultant on organisational development for the women's community and voluntary sectors in Ireland, while researching a doctoral thesis on women's community education in relation to the promotion of social justice and equality for women in Ireland, North and South.

FR PETER MCVERRY SJ grew up in Newry, County Down. In 1962, he entered the Jesuit Order and was ordained in 1975. He worked as a priest in the inner city in Dublin from 1975 to 1980, where he encountered some homeless

children. He opened a hostel for homeless children in 1979 and this subsequently became his life work. He moved to Ballymun in 1980 and opened three more hostels, a residential drug detox centre for homeless people and two drug-free after-care houses. He has written on many issues relating to young homeless people, such as accommodation, drugs, juvenile justice, the gardaí, the prisons and education. He has a regular article in the monthly Redemptorist magazine *Reality* and speaks on issues of homelessness, justice and faith to groups around the country. He has produced a book of writings entitled *The Meaning Is in the Shadows*. His most recent book is entitled *Jesus – Social Revolutionary?*. He has been a critic of government policy on issues such as homelessness, drugs and criminal justice.

DR MAURICE MANNING is president of the Irish Human Rights Commission. An academic by background, Dr Manning previously lectured in politics in University College Dublin and has been visiting professor at the University of Paris (Vincennes) and the University of West Florida. He is a member of the senate of the National University of Ireland and of the governing authority of University College Dublin and has been a member of the governing authority of the European University Institute at Florence. Dr Manning has written several books on modern Irish politics. He was a member of the Oireachtas for twenty-one years, serving in both the Dáil and the Seanad. He has been a member of the New Ireland Forum and the British Inter-Parliamentary Body. He has served as both leader of the Seanad and leader of the Opposition in that House.

DR DIARMUID MARTIN, Archbishop of Dublin, was born in Dublin on 8 April 1945. He studied philosophy at University College Dublin and theology at the Dublin Diocesan Seminary. He was ordained as a priest on 25 May

1969. During his service at the Pontifical Council for Justice and Peace, Archbishop Martin represented the Holy See at the major United Nations conferences on social questions in the 1990s. He also participated in activities of the World Bank and the International Monetary Fund, especially on the theme of international debt and poverty reduction. In March 2001, he was elevated to the rank of archbishop and undertook responsibilities as Permanent Observer of the Holy See in Geneva, at the United Nations Office and Specialised Agencies and at the World Trade Organization. He was appointed Coadjutor Archbishop of Dublin on 3 May 2003. He succeeded Cardinal Desmond Connell as Archbishop of Dublin on 26 April 2004.

MARGARET MARTIN is the director of Women's Aid in Dublin. Women's Aid is a feminist, campaigning and political organisation that, for more than thirty years, has been working towards and is committed to the elimination of violence against women. Women's Aid provides direct support services and information to thousands of women experiencing male violence and abuse through the National Freephone Domestic Violence Helpline, and one-to-one support services. Women's Aid works to raise awareness of the prevalence of physical, emotional and sexual violence against women in Irish society. Most recently, Women's Aid has worked to highlight the number of women murdered in Ireland, and the strong risk factor domestic violence plays in such murders.

SALOME MBUGUA is a native of Kenya and has been living in Ireland for the past fourteen years. She has eighteen years' experience of working with disadvantaged and marginalised groups, especially women, children and young people in Kenya, Uganda and Ireland. Her background is in social work and community development. She is an activist and advocate of human rights, justice and gender equality.

JOHN MONAGHAN has been a volunteer member of the Society of St Vincent de Paul in his home parish of Leixlip, County Kildare, for nearly twenty-five years. He is currently a national vice-president of the SVP with particular responsibility for social policy and justice and acts as media spokesperson on issues related to these areas. In 2006, he was appointed by the then Minister of Social and Family Affairs to the board of the Combat Poverty Agency. He has been married to Catherine for over thirty-six years and they have three grown-up children. In his day job, he is a professor of Mechanical Engineering and a Fellow at Trinity College, Dublin.

A true giant of the modern game, **SEÁN ÓG Ó HAILPÍN** plays for the Cork senior hurlers. He has the rare distinction of holding minor, Under-21 and senior All-Ireland medals, including three of the latter in 1999, 2004 and 2005, when he captained the side. 2004 saw him sweep the boards personally as he was named Vodafone Hurler of the Year, GPA Hurler of the Year and Texaco Hurler of the Year. He achieved a hat trick of All-Star awards in 2003, 2004 and 2005 and has also won two county championships with his club, Na Piarsaigh. A dual player who has previously represented the Cork senior footballers, he took part in the International Rules series against Australia in 2004 and 2005.

DONNCHA O'CONNELL is the senior Irish member of FRALEX, the legal expert group that advises the EU Fundamental Rights Agency based in Vienna. From 2005 to 2008 he was the Dean of Law at NUI Galway, where he continues to teach the following subjects in the School of Law: Constitutional Law, European Human Rights, Processes of Law Reform and Equality Law: Principles and Thematic Application. He was the first full-time director of the Irish Council for Civil Liberties from 1999 to 2002, after which he was appointed to the EU Network of Independent Experts on Fundamental Rights. In the past he has served as a member of the National Council of the Free Legal Advice Centres (FLAC) Ltd and the Executive Committee of Amnesty International Ireland. He is the editor of the *Irish Human Rights Law Review* (Clarus Press) and a member of the board of directors of the Druid Theatre Company.

JACK O'CONNOR has served as the general president of SIPTU, Ireland's largest trade union, since 2003 and was re-elected unopposed in 2006. He has been a member of the executive council of the Irish Congress of Trade Unions since 2001 and was elected as vice-president of Congress in 2007. He also serves on both the General Purposes Committee and the Private Sector Committee of the ICTU. He participated on the ICTU negotiating team for the Sustaining Progress and Towards 2016 agreements. His declared priorities are combating worker exploitation, promoting people's right to participate in collective bargaining, advancing the training and skills agenda and asserting the economic, as well as the moral, superiority of fairness at work and justice in society.

COLM O'GORMAN was appointed executive director of Amnesty International Ireland in November 2007. He previously worked as a psychotherapist and was the founder and former director of One in Four, the national non-governmental organisation that supports women and men who have experienced sexual violence. In this role, Colm was instrumental in the establishment of the Ferns Inquiry, the first state investigation into clerical sexual abuse. He has been widely credited with bringing an objective and pioneering approach to the sensitive and challenging issues around the Irish experience of sexual violence. He also served as a member of the Seanad. His work as a human rights defender is driven by a deep commitment to human rights and social justice and an abiding belief in the power of advocacy and activism, which challenges all of us to use our individual and collective voices to demand change where it is most needed.

EMILY O'REILLY was appointed Ireland's third Ombudsman on 1 June 2003, by the President of Ireland, Mrs Mary McAleese, on the nomination of both Houses of the Oireachtas (Dáil and Seanad). Prior to her appointment, she was a journalist and author and had been a political correspondent for various media outlets since 1989. The new ombudsman was also appointed Ireland's second Information Commissioner, under the Freedom of Information Act 1997, on 1 June 2003. In her role as commissioner, Emily O'Reilly provides an independent review of decisions relating to the right of access of members of the public to records held by public bodies. In addition, under the European Communities (Access to Information on the Environment) Regulations, S.I. 133 of 2007, Emily O'Reilly (as holder of the Office of Information Commissioner) was assigned the legally separate role of Commissioner for Environmental Information. Her role is to decide appeals taken by members of the public who are not satisfied with the outcome of their requests to public authorities for environmental information. She is also an ex-officio member of the Standards in Public Office Commission, the Dáil Constituency Commission, the Commission for Public Service Appointments and the Referendum Commission. Emily O'Reilly is a native of Tullamore, County Offaly, and is married with five children. She was educated at University College Dublin and Trinity College, Dublin and was the recipient of a Nieman Fellowship in Journalism at Harvard University in Cambridge. In June 2008, she was elected chairperson of the British and Irish Ombudsman Association. In December 2008, the National University of Ireland presented the ombudsman with the honorary degree, Doctor of Laws, in recognition of her contribution to public service and to human rights.

JOHN SAUNDERS has been the director of Shine (formerly Schizophrenia Ireland-Lucia Foundation) since 2001. As director of Shine, he is specifically responsible for the development of accurate public awareness of schizophrenia and related mental disorders and highlighting the issues and concerns of people with a diagnosis and their caring families. He was a member of the National Expert Group to review and update the mental health services, which was established by the Minister of State at the Department of Health and Children, as well as the NESF Working Group on Mental Health and Social Inclusion. He is a member of the board of directors of EUFAMI (a European organisation of voluntary mental health associations representing families). He currently serves on the Mental Health Commission as well as the Health Service Executive Implementation Group overseeing the development of *A Vision for Change* – the new national mental health policy. He is a member of the National Disability Authority Mental Health Advisory Group and is the current chair of the Action on Suicide Alliance and of the Irish Mental Health Coalition.

Born in Dublin in 1952, **DEREK SPEIRS** worked in a photofinishing laboratory in Tallaght for a couple of years after leaving school. He then moved to London and studied at the Polytechnic of Central London, obtaining a BA CNAA and The Royal College of Art, London receiving a MA RCA. He began his professional career as a photographer in London in 1977, working with the Report co-operative of photographers with the founder of Report, Simon Guttmann. In 1978 he returned to Dublin and established an agency along similar lines, also operating under the name of Report. It specialised in the coverage of politics, current affairs, theatre and the arts, the activities of the labour movement and collaborative work with NGOs and marginalised groups. He also taught in the National College of Art and Design, Dublin for a period in 1978 and 1979.

His photographs are published regularly in the national and international press. His work has been included in exhibitions on topical social issues, including *Speirs at Large* (1988) which toured Ireland and east Berlin, and *At Work* (1994) an Irish Museum of Modern Art exhibition dealing with the changing nature of work, with a commentary by writer Gene Kerrigan. His books include *Goodbye to All That* (1992), which covered the Ireland of Charles Haughey, with text by Gene Kerrigan.

DR KATHERINE ZAPPONE is an educator and independent researcher. Appointed by the Minister for Justice, she has served as a commissioner on the Irish Human Rights Commission since 2001. She taught Practical Theology for a decade in Trinity College, Dublin, has lectured widely throughout Australia, Canada, Europe and the United States and has written extensively on matters related to ethics, spirituality, equality and human rights. She learned the art of public policy as chief executive of the National Women's Council of Ireland. She is a co-founder of An Cosán, a large community-based organisation in Dublin committed to eradicating poverty through education. She has worked with Atlantic Philanthropies on their Children's Programme, establishing the Tallaght West Childhood Development Initiative, Ltd to implement a ten-year strategy to promote children's well-being. She has recently published memoirs, *Our Lives Out Loud: In Pursuit of Justice and Equality* (Dublin: O'Brien Press) with her married partner, Dr Ann Louise Gilligan. The memoirs document their reasons for taking a case of public interest against the Irish state for legal recognition of their Canadian marriage. She holds a PhD in Education and Religion from Boston College.

INDEX